bake

favourite home-made recipes

PENGUIN BOOKS

Published by the Penguin Group

Penguin Group (NZ), 67 Apollo Drive, Rosedale,
North Shore 0632, New Zealand (a division of Pearson New Zealand Ltd)
Penguin Group (USA) Inc., 375 Hudson Street,
New York, New York 10014, USA
Penguin Group (Canada), 90 Eglinton Avenue East, Suite 700, Toronto,
Ontario, M4P 2Y3, Canada (a division of Pearson Penguin Canada Inc.)
Penguin Books Ltd, 80 Strand, London, WC2R 0RL, England
Penguin Ireland, 25 St Stephen's Green,
Dublin 2, Ireland (a division of Penguin Books Ltd)
Penguin Group (Australia), 250 Camberwell Road, Camberwell,
Victoria 3124, Australia (a division of Pearson Australia Group Pty Ltd)
Penguin Books India Pvt Ltd, 11, Community Centre,
Panchsheel Park, New Delhi – 110 017, India
Penguin Books (South Africa) (Pty) Ltd, 24 Sturdee Avenue,
Rosebank, Johannesburg 2196, South Africa

Penguin Books Ltd, Registered Offices: 80 Strand, London, WC2R 0RL, England

First published by Penguin Group (NZ), 2009
 5 7 9 10 8 6

Copyright © Allyson Gofton 2009

Photography by Alan Gillard
Designed and typeset by seven.co.nz
Prepress by Image Centre Ltd
Printed in China through Bookbuilders, Hong Kong

Publisher Alison Brook
Managing editor Andrea Coppock

Assistants – Mary-Lou McGarry, Olwen Edwards, Ann Boardman and Tonita Thorpe
Thanks to Sabato, Mt. Eden, Auckland, for Rachel Carley crockery
Thanks to Chris Beckett and Jean Colbeck for crockery

ISBN 978 0 14 301170 5

A catalogue record for this book is available
from the National Library of New Zealand.

www.penguin.co.nz

bake
allyson gofton

favourite home-made recipes

Penguin Books

For Jean-Luc and Olive-Rose

'A house is beautiful not because of its
walls, but because of its cakes.'

— Old Russian Proverb

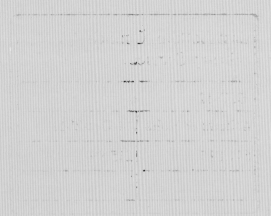

contents

Whenever I begin to gather the items and ingredients for baking, I am reminded of love.

It might come from knowing I'm cooking up my Mother's favourite tea cake recipe to serve to girlfriends; it might be from thinking about how my Godmother taught me to make her shortbread recipe and would always bake it for me when I wandered home after some far-away travel; it might be from my uncle, a chef and actor, who savoured much of his life in Spain and returned home with Moorish-spiced baking to tempt a cooking-mad niece; or it might be because I always smile, remembering how my Grandmother would not allow anyone to flush the old pull-chain loo when she popped a hand-whisked sponge into the ancient oven that stood on the stone floor of her basement flat lest it collapsed.

Baking is about loving, about sharing and about giving as much as it is about cooking. Nothing fills a house with joy as much as freshly baked goods – baking marks a celebration, helps alleviate sad news, fills a child's empty tummy after a busy play day and revives lagging spirits or energy when we are tired. Baking comes from the heart, no matter how simple or involved. This book contains my most treasured recipes, some of which I have reworked to make them even more fail-proof and delicious, and all of which I love to bake whenever I can. There are plenty of tips, hints, variations and reference material to help you have success whenever you bake.

Enjoy

Allyson

baking
made
simple

essential ingredients

With Bake, I've tried to stick to the sort of baking supplies found in most pantries and kitchens. Yes, of course, there are the unexpected flavours, spices or toppings that come out on special occasions, but I feel it's important that you can make virtually every recipe in this book with what you have at hand.

This section outlines pantry basics and equipment you need for successful baking. Having the right tools for the job makes a big difference to the end result!

flours

White flour comes in two grades and both are important to have in your pantry. Pure or standard flour has been used for most recipes in this book. It is an all-purpose 'soft' flour, best for baking biscuits, cakes, slices, loaves, muffins, etc. Where more structure is required, as in bread or yeast baking or heavy fruit cakes, I use high grade flour. It has a higher protein (gluten) content.

Self-raising flour has had a raising agent added by the miller, which saves the cook adding baking powder to non-self-raising flours. However, it does not have a long shelf life, due to the raising agent absorbing damp from the atmosphere, causing loss of its raising properties.

Although the ratio of raising agent in self-raising flours may differ slightly from brand to brand, for home-baking, the rule of thumb is 1–1½ teaspoons of baking powder to 1 cup of plain or high grade flour; often there will be a recipe on the flour packet which will give you a clue as to the recommended ratio for the particular product.

Wholemeal flour contains all parts of the wheat grain – bran, germ and endosperm. Extra water may be required in a recipe when using wholemeal flour, as bran will absorb more water than plain flour does. Use wholemeal flour for bread, buns, rolls, shortbread, cakes and biscuits. Wholemeal flour can become rancid in our warm climate so buy and use within a reasonable period of time and store away from sunlight.

Wheatgerm flour is white flour with added wheatgerm.

Stoneground flour has been ground in the traditional way, between two stones, hence the name. It will give a crunchier, coarser and heavier texture. It might be best to mix it half and half with white or wholemeal flour. It will become rancid quickly, so keep in a cool place. If converting a recipe that uses white flour, you will need to allow more liquid.

Semolina is made from hard durum wheat and is usually milled fairly coarsely, which is how we generally recognise it. However, finer semolina flour is available and can be used in the making of pasta, gnocchi and other baked goods.

Gluten-free flour blends are now readily available from a number of producers. Most are blends of different grains to achieve a palatable and appealing result. Blends include rice, potato, tapioca, soy, buckwheat or cornflour. Be aware that some gluten-free flours are baking mixes and include raising agents. Check the label to see if a gluten-free baking powder will need to be added. See page 115 for a general purpose gluten-free flour mix.

Buckwheat flour is technically not a grain and as such is gluten free. It belongs to the rhubarb family, has a very strong flavour and can be difficult to digest. Use in conjunction with flour in baking quick breads like pancakes, pikelets, scones and muffins for a flavour change.

Cornflour is great for those with wheat allergies, but make sure you look for true maize cornflour and not wheaten cornflour. In baking it creates a more fragile biscuit or shortbread and in cakes, a finer crumb.

Nut flours are now readily available. Look for walnut, hazelnut and chestnut flour, and ground almonds, also known as almond meal.

Rice flour can be purchased in white or brown and tends to produce a crumbly result. This can be lessened by substituting one part arrowroot or other thickener to four parts rice flour. As rice flour absorbs more moisture, more liquid may be required. It is also a good substitute for thickening gravy, sauces and custards.

Soy flour is prepared from roasted soy beans and is rich in high quality protein, though it has a strong and distinctive nut-like flavour. Because baking with soy flour has a tendency to brown more quickly than wheat baking, you may have to either reduce the baking time or lower the temperature slightly. Soy can replace up to one-quarter of any wheat flour, but the liquid may have to be upped a little.

Measuring flour
All flours should be spooned lightly into the cup and levelled off with the straight back edge of a knife. **Do not** pack flour firmly into a cup.

allyson's tips

'0' and '00' flours
- These numbers are used on imported flours (usually Italian) to designate how finely they have been milled. '00' is used for fresh pasta and cakes, and '0' is to bake bread.

- In America cornflour is called cornstarch. When used as a thickener to make custards or sauces, cornflour has twice the thickening properties of flour. Cook well though to avoid a chalky taste.

Storing flour
- Flour should be stored in an airtight container away from direct sunlight and excessive heat so that it does not dry out. This causes it to become stale and changes the liquid to flour ratio in recipes.

raising agents

Baking powder is a mixture of cream of tartar (acidic) and baking soda (alkaline) and has a little starch or flour added to stabilise the mixture and prevent caking, though gluten-free baking powder is now available. Baking powder will not last forever, so throw it away if it's over 12 months old.

To make your own, the ratio for baking powder is 1 part baking soda and 2 parts cream of tartar. Store in an airtight container.

Cream of tartar is the acidic ingredient in baking powder – keep in an airtight container.

Baking soda, also called bicarbonate of soda in overseas cookbooks, is the alkaline ingredient in baking powder. It requires an acidic ingredient in order to work and in some recipes where an acidic ingredient is used such as sour cream, recipes may only call for baking soda. Keep in an airtight container. It is best to dissolve in liquid or sift with dry ingredients before incorporating into a recipe.

yeast

Surebake yeast mix is active dry yeast with dough improvers added. Active yeast is dried yeast granules. I prefer to 'sponge' both varieties, even though at times recipes on the back of packets do not recommend this step, to ensure the yeast is alive and active. As a general rule 3 teaspoons of Surebake yeast mix is equivalent to 1 teaspoon active yeast granules.

eggs

The size of eggs can make a huge difference to your baking. In recent years the selection of eggs has increased. Often, too, they no longer carry a size, but a qualifying statement. I have used size 7 eggs throughout, unless otherwise stated.

Here's a guide:
Medium Size 5 = 44 grams
Standard Size 6 = 53 grams
Large Size 7 = 62 grams
Jumbo = 68 grams

They fetched him first the sweetest wine,
Then mead in mazers they combine
With lots of royal spice
And gingerbread, exceeding fine,
And liqourice and eglantyne
and sugar, very nice
– Chaucer

sugars

White sugar is the most commonly used sugar. It is highly processed, pure white and has even crystals perfect for baking and preserves.

Caster sugar is so named as it is milled fine enough to use in a sugar caster or sprinkler. Caster sugar dissolves quickly making it ideal for meringues, pavlovas and fine baking (sponge cakes, etc.). In American recipe books, the term superfine sugar may be used.

Icing sugar is formed from fine grains of sugar that are crushed to a powder to make the smoothest sugar of all. It is also called 'confectioner's sugar' or 'powdered sugar'. Occasionally, some starch is added to keep it from forming clumps, though gluten-free icing sugar is now available. Keep well sealed in a dry place.

Raw/golden granulated sugar can be used as an alternative to white granulated sugar when a warm flavour is wanted.

Light/soft brown sugar is prepared from caster sugar mixed with a dark sugar syrup (gained during the refining process). Ideal for both savoury and sweet baking where it adds a warm depth of flavour. When measuring brown sugar, always pack firmly into a cup.

Demerara sugar takes its name from the town where it was first produced in Guyana. When used in baking, its firm crystal offers a warm note and often a crisp crust.

Dark cane sugar/muscovado is very dark moist sugar and is prepared much the same way as soft brown sugar, only molasses is added back to the finely milled sugar, giving it a distinctive rich almost bitter flavour. The name muscovado comes from the Spanish *más acabado*, meaning 'more finished'.

Molasses sugar is the darkest of all sugars, containing the highest amount of molasses syrup. It is the best choice where richness and depth of flavour is paramount, e.g. gingerbreads, Christmas cakes, rich fruit puddings and cakes. It can also be used where jaggery is called for in ethnic dishes. Molasses is the by-product from the refining of sugar from the sugar cane.

Jaggery/palm sugar has deep brown to soft honey hues, warm, caramel flavours and a fudge-like texture. It is prepared from the sap of various palm trees that, once collected, is boiled and stirred to become fudge-like before setting in moulds. It needs to be grated or crumbled to use and should be kept in an airtight container so it does not become too brittle.

fats

Butter provides a superior flavour in baking. If you use margarine, look for one with a minimum fat content of 81%. Lite margarines may work, depending on the recipe, but products labelled 'table spreads' or similar will not – their fat content is too low.

Many professional cooks and some writers call for unsalted butter for baking, but this can be an expensive option. Unsalted butter will offer a somewhat sweeter taste to your baking. You will notice a taste difference in items like shortbreads or in baking where good quality chocolate is being used. Otherwise standard creamery butter is perfect.

Oils are called for in place of butter in some recipes. In recipes where butter is melted, you can substitute oil. Use a flavourless oil such as canola, light olive or grapeseed oil in baking, unless a nut oil is called for. Oil should be purchased in a dark coloured bottle and stored in a cool place away from light and heat to prevent the oil from becoming rancid. Nut oils are particularly prone to rancidity so use soon after opening.

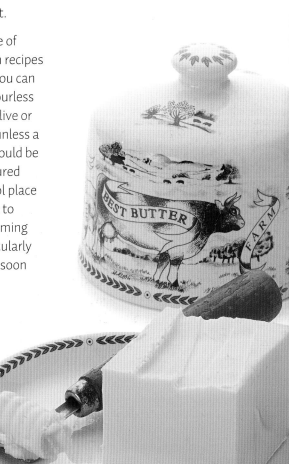

syrups

Many of the syrups that we cook with are by-products of the starch industry and add flavour to our foods. Most are inter-changeable; though the darker the syrup, the stronger and often more bitter the flavour.

Sugar syrups

Golden syrup is a light coloured syrup obtained from sugar cane during the refining process and is much-loved in Kiwi baking for the warm caramel flavour it gives to baked foods.

Treacle is also from sugar cane, but is darker and more intense in flavour. Use in gingerbread cakes for a classic flavour.

Molasses is the darkest syrup obtained from sugar refining. There are a number of grades of molasses with the lowest grade being black-strap molasses.

Other syrups

Apple syrup is prepared from the juice of crushed apples and is boiled to reach syrup consistency. Delicious used with pip fruits in baked foods.

Corn syrup is a thick sweet syrup prepared from cornflour with an enzyme added. It has the great benefit of inhibiting crystallisation hence its use in recipes for icings, preserves and confectionery.

Glucose has many sources: sugar cane, corn or even grape sugar. Like corn syrup it does not crystallise easily and so it is used in confectionery, baking and more.

Maple syrup is prepared from the sap or water collected from the maple tree. For true maple syrup, look for products with the Canadian maple leaf on them. Beware of those labelled maple-flavoured syrup as they are not authentic, they are only flavoured syrups and their flavour is poor at best. Use in place of golden syrup.

milks, creams and yoghurts

Throughout the book, I have used blue-topped or light blue milk for cooking, though on most occasions, green milk will be perfectly acceptable. If the milk is being heated for say custard, use blue milk to avoid any possibility of curdling from other ingredients.

Full fat cream, 35% fat, was always used. Be aware that light cream will not whip, but is fine to use in custard recipes.

Where yoghurt was used I chose plain, thick Greek-style yoghurt for its creamy flavour and smooth texture. If using a thin, pourable yoghurt, you may have a slightly different end result with a sharper taste.

Soy milk can be substituted in all recipes.

The owl and the pussy cat

The Owl and the Pussy Cat went to sea
In a beautiful pea-green boat,
They took some honey, and plenty of money,
Wrapped up in a five pound note.

– Edward Lear, 19th century
English poet, artist and writer.

allyson's tip

Measuring honey and syrups
When measuring syrups, heat the measuring spoon first – the syrup will run off with ease. For cup measures, lightly grease the cup to make removing all the syrup easy. And, if you have time, stand the can or bottle of syrup (with the lid opened) in a warm sink of water to reduce its viscosity, making measuring much easier.

honey

Each honey style offers a totally different flavour to your baking, so choose one that suits the recipe.

Sheer flavoured honeys are lighter coloured honeys and best used for desserts and lighter style cakes. Try vipers bugloss, nodding thistle, blue borage, South Island clover (creamed or runny), tawari, lavender or rose honey.

Mellow flavoured honeys are warmer toned and ideal for most baking. Try orange blossom, manuka, rata, pohutukawa, North Island clover and avocado honey.

Strong flavoured honeys are darker, pungent and best in rich fruit cakes and gingerbreads. Try rewarewa, wild thyme (South Island), honeydew, kamahi and bush blends.

dried and glacé fruits

Dried fruits are usually stoned and dried, either naturally under the sun or through mechanical means. Many dried fruit mixes and some individual mixes are then coated lightly in a sugar or glucose syrup, which makes them very shiny. This is not essential to flavour and adds additional, often unwanted, sweetness.

Glacé is the French word for glazed, and the term applies to fruit that has been preserved in a sugar syrup and then further glazed with syrup.

Crystallised fruit is sugar-soaked preserved fruit coated with sugar and while, strictly speaking, glacé is the shiny sugar syrup coating on cherries, the two terms are more or less interchangeable these days.

Dried fruits
Keep a selection on hand to add variety to your baking.

Currants, raisins and sultanas are all dried grapes of different varieties. **Currants** are small black seedless grapes, **raisins** are dried red grapes, sometimes seedless, while **muscatels** are dessert raisins, often with seeds and dried on their stems, they are a delicious treat. **Sultanas** are dried small white seedless grapes. Dried **cranberries,** also sold as Craisins (brand name), add a sharpness when used,

while **blueberries** add both an interesting colour and intense sweet flavour. **Prunes** are dried plums – look for plump juicy prunes and for ease, buy stoned. **Dates** come both dried and fresh. For easy use, look for stoned, dried dates and soak them before adding to a cake or scone mix to ensure good flavour and texture when eating.

There are now more lighter coloured dried fruits available and they make a sensational change to traditional fruit minces and puddings. Buy New Zealand **apricots** for flavour, nothing beats them. Dried **apples** are delicious when soaked in a favourite alcohol and used in a cake – use soon after buying lest they become brown and shrivelled. Dried **peaches, nectarines** and **cherries** are sensational in flavour, try in a friand or muffin for a change. Dried **bananas** are brown and discoloured, but make an interesting addition to a banana bread, while dried **figs** and **figlets** (small whole figs) can be anything from light brown to almost black and **mango** slices can be coloured bright orange and can be very chewy.

Glacé fruits
Glacé **cherries** – both red and green – are double-dosed, having been candied and then glazed, which explains why they

are so sticky. To stop them sinking to the bottom of cakes in baking, they can be rinsed and dried before adding to the cake mix. **Mixed peel** – lemon and orange peel – has become rather sugary and flavourless, so look for quality mixed peel for special baking. Look for whole glacé **oranges** to decorate a special cake. **Papaya** can be quite chewy and intensely sweet. **Pineapple, citron, melon** and **guava** strips, **kiwifruit** slices, **quince** chunks, **figs, pear, apricot** and **peach** halves are also available.

Crystallised fruits
Crystallised **ginger** and **angelica** are survivors of the popular confections of the past. Pair ginger with chocolate or lemon and use angelica as a garnish. New and interesting are crystallised **strawberries** – ideal in biscotti.

coconut

Desiccated coconut is the dried white meat of the coconut. It is graded after processing – the finest grade is 'macaroon', but also includes flakes and threads. Keep coconut in the freezer as, like nuts, it has a high fat content and will become rancid in our warm kitchens, especially if opened and not sealed properly.

Coconut cream and milk are both made by pouring boiling water over the grated coconut flesh, then squeezing and straining the resulting pulp when it is cool. The amount of water added determines whether it is cream, which is thicker, or milk and if the same pulp is used several times, it will produce a progressively less rich milk each time. Coconut milk, which also can be made from desiccated coconut, makes an interesting addition to a recipe, when used in place of milk.

'He who plants a coconut tree plants food and drink, vessels and clothing, a home for himself and a heritage for his children.'

– South Seas saying

nuts

To avoid nuts that are rancid, buy them from shops where there is a good turnover of product. Most nuts can be interchanged in recipes. Once bought, nuts are best stored in the freezer as they have a high oil content that will become rancid quickly in our warm climate. To refreshen, lightly toast the nuts – this will also enhance their flavour.

allyson's tips

Roasting and grinding

• Roasted nuts offer a warmer flavour in baking. Place nuts on a baking tray and roast at 180 °C for 8–12 minutes. Smaller nuts such as pine nuts require less time, while hazelnuts and Brazil nuts take longer. Check regularly when roasting.

• Roasted nuts should not be processed while they are warm because they will form a paste.

• If you are processing your own nuts to a powder, 1¼ cups of whole nuts will make up 1 cup ground. Pulse in a food processor for best results.

flavourings

Vanilla has become incredibly fashionable of late. It is available as an essence, extract, pod, paste or powder. Extracts and pure vanilla essences are the finest quality, with imitation vanilla essence a poor second. Having said that, for everyday family baking it is perfectly okay. Thick black vanilla paste or ground vanilla powders are intensely fragrant, while vanilla pods will add a subtle note.

Almond, like vanilla, comes as an extract or essence. It is prepared from bitter almonds and the extract is intensely flavoured, so use sparingly.

Citrus and fruit have come to market and make adding that lemon or orange zest so much easier. Keep away from sunlight and heat.

spices

Pantry basics
I have a penchant for spices and keep many to hand. For a basic baking spice pantry, have on hand: ground cardamom, cinnamon, cloves, mixed spice, ginger, mace and/or nutmeg. To add extra flair to your baking, include cassia, coriander (yes, it adds subtleness to spice mixes), star anise and a batch of my apple pie spice to use where apples and pears are included in the baking.

Apple Pie Spice
Mix together:
1½ tablespoons ground
    coriander
2 teaspoons ground cinnamon
1 teaspoon ground cardamom
½ teaspoon each of ground
    nutmeg, mace, allspice,
    ginger and cloves
Keep in an airtight container.

baking with the food processor

The food processor is an enclosed unit and as a result less air will be incorporated.

To achieve a good result using a food processor, begin by processing the eggs and sugar until creamy. Add the softened butter and process again until well mixed and creamy. This will avoid a thick butter and sugar mass collecting under the blade.

Then pulse in the liquid ingredients and layer the sifted dry ingredients, nuts, coconut, fruit or whatever 'tender' ingredients are being used on top and pulse to combine. Do not process as the end result will be tough, less likely to rise and the 'tender' ingredients pulverised.

substitutions

If you have started baking and find you are missing an ingredient, it doesn't necessarily mean an emergency dash to the shop. Here are a few substitutions that you can make.

Caster sugar Place 1 cup plus 2 tablespoons granulated sugar in a food processor and pulse for approximately 1 minute until the grains are finer.

Dark brown sugar 1 cup dark brown sugar = 1 cup caster sugar plus ¼ cup treacle or golden syrup.

Light brown sugar 1 cup light brown sugar = 1 cup caster sugar plus 2 tablespoons golden syrup.

Buttermilk 1 cup buttermilk = ½ cup plain non-fat yoghurt plus ½ cup milk.

Sour cream 1 cup sour cream = 1 cup milk with 1 tablespoon lemon juice or white vinegar stirred through and allowed to stand for 5 minutes to sour.

Milk 1 cup blue or light blue milk = ½ cup water and ½ cup evaporated milk or cream. Or use soy milk.

Baking powder 1 teaspoon baking powder = ¼ teaspoon baking soda plus ½ cup buttermilk or sour milk and reduce the liquid in the recipe by ½ cup. Alternatively, mix 2 teaspoons cream of tartar and 1 teaspoon baking soda. Use 1 teaspoon of this mixture. Add a pinch of flour if storing to prevent caking.

Self-raising flour 1 cup self-raising flour = 1 cup plain flour plus 1½ teaspoons baking powder.

Butter 250 grams butter = the same quantity in margarine or ⅞ cup oil, if the recipe called for the butter to be melted.

Egg 1 whole egg = 2 egg yolks plus 1 tablespoon water.

Honey 1 cup honey = 1 cup plus 2 tablespoons of sugar plus ¼ cup of the same liquid used in the recipe.

Lemon juice Small amounts such as 1 teaspoon can be substituted with vinegar. 1 teaspoon lemon juice = ½ teaspoon vinegar.

equipment

cake tins

Choose good quality cake, muffin, patty tins and the like. The better the quality, the longer their lifetime. Lighter coloured tins will reflect the heat and will produce lighter crusted baking, while darker tins retain the heat and the finished product will have a darker, thicker crust. If you have darker tins and you find your cakes or baking has a darker crumb than you like, consider lowering the temperature a little, by 20–25 °C. If you prefer non-stick, be aware that once they become scratched, they will stick.

Prepare the tins as per the instructions in the recipes for the best results and wash the tins lightly in warm water. Dry well by placing in a warm oven to avoid rusting. Dishwashers are not the place for cake tins as they rarely remove stubborn baked-on bits and in the damp steaming environment cake tins will rust.

allyson's tips

• Use the tin size specified in the recipe. A different tin size may result in a disappointing end result. Cake and loaf tins are measured from the base of the tin not the top.

Substituting shapes
• If you want to use a cake tin that is a different shape from the one in the recipe, substitute one with the same liquid capacity – you can test this by filling them with water.

preparing cake tins

Follow the recipe instructions to ensure baking comes away easily from the tin.

Grease and flour
Lightly grease the tin with melted butter, margarine or oil and then sprinkle in a little flour. To make sure the sides and base are evenly covered, tap the tin while turning it around. Tip out any excess flour. This method will leave a light crust around the edge.

Grease and line
Lightly grease the tin with melted butter, margarine or oil. Line the base with baking paper and, if wished, the sides too. I usually line the base only, unless making a heavy fruit cake, or one with a large amount of sugar.

Grease only
For sponge cake mixes, only grease the tins so that you achieve a golden crust and not a steamed, moist base and sides.

the baking basics

If you are just starting out baking for your home it is nice to have several tin sizes to choose from. These are the main ones to have:

- 1 standard muffin tray (has 12 muffin cups)
- round 20-cm cake tin (preferably with interchangeable ring tin base)
- Swiss roll tin or slice tin (20 cm x 30 cm)
- 1–2 loaf or bread tins
- square 20-cm cake tin (can be used for slices)
- 23-cm loose-bottom flan tin
- 1–2 baking trays

Loaf tins once were standard sizes, but this no longer is the case. The three main sizes used in this book relate to cup capacity.

- Small loaf tin (18 cm x 8 cm) = 5 cup capacity
- Medium loaf tin (22 cm x 9 cm) = 6 cup capacity
- Large loaf tin (21 cm x 11 cm) = 7 cup capacity (this tin is very deep and called a bread loaf tin)

Substitutions should be made on a capacity size. To measure, fill the tins with water.

general equipment

The vast majority of recipes in this book have been prepared with a bowl and wooden spoon and a few other basics – here's a list of basic requirements:

- 1 set NZ standard measuring spoons
- 1 set NZ standard measuring cups
- 1–2 Pyrex jugs – 1 small and 1 large size, to measure liquid ingredients
- 2–3 wooden spoons
- 1 large metal spoon – the thin edge is better for mixing
- 1 large slotted metal spoon – the holes assist with folding
- 2 thin-bladed plastic spatulas or scrapers – dishwasher-proof are best
- 1 large sieve – for sifting dry ingredients
- 1 long palette knife – for lifting and moving goods and icing
- 1 small palette knife – great for icing
- 1 rolling pin – wooden is best
- 1 citrus grater (zester)
- 1 lemon squeezer
- 1 peeler
- 1 paring knife – plus a serrated paring knife, if possible
- 1–2 glazing brushes – for glazing and greasing
- 1 balloon or egg whisk
- 1 pair scissors
- 1–2 cake racks – to cool baking on
- 1 set electric hand-held beaters – makes beating cream and eggs easy

Nice to have but not essential

- A food processor and/or a mix master (Kenwood or Kitchen Aid-style)
- A cherry stoner
- An icing bag with nozzles
- Double saucepan, though a Pyrex bowl and a saucepan will suffice
- Biscuit forcer (press)

bowls

Have a selection of bowls, all microwave-proof. Buy the best you can afford. Old-style Mason Cash crockery bowls will last a lifetime – they are microwave-proof, stay firmly on the table when being used, wash well in a dishwasher, are easy to hold when beating and are wide brimmed making them good for beating egg whites and cream where you need to incorporate air. And a couple of good old-fashioned Pyrex bowls are ideal – they act as a double saucepan and are generally great to have at hand.

ovens

Oven temperature is critical to ensuring successful baking outcomes. New ovens will vary to old ones, so it is wise to run a couple of well-loved recipes through a new oven to get a handle on how it performs.

You must preheat your oven to the temprature stated in the recipe, before you put the baking in the oven.

All recipes in this book were cooked on 'bake' (not fan-bake, see Allyson's tip) unless otherwise stated.

allyson's tip

Fan-baking
If you are cooking two tins or trays at the same time, use the fan-bake option. You will need to drop the temperature by 20 °C.

measurements

Throughout this book New Zealand standard measures have been used.

1 cup = 250 millilitres
1 tablespoon = 15 millilitres
1 teaspoon = 5 millilitres

Please note: If cooking from an Australian cookbook the Australian tablespoon = 20 millilitres.

All measures are level and not 'heaped', 'scant' or 'rounded'.

To measure dry goods, spoon into cup, do not pack down; level off moving the back of a knife across the cup. The only exception is when measuring brown sugar – pack it firmly into the cup. The mound will hold its shape when turned out.

measurement conversions

A general guide for goods used in this book, converted from measures to weights. Please note they are rounded to the nearest 5 or 10 grams.

Butter

1 cup	250 grams
(firmly packed)	
½ cup	125 grams
1 tablespoon	15 grams

Oil

1 cup	220 grams
½ cup	110 grams

Flour

1 cup	125 grams
½ cup	65 grams
¼ cup	30 grams

Breadcrumbs – fresh

1 cup	70 grams

Coconut – desiccated

1 cup	90 grams
½ cup	45 grams

Nuts – walnuts

1 cup	100 grams
½ cup	50 grams

Nuts – pistachios

1 cup	130 grams
½ cup	65 grams

Nuts – hazelnuts

1 cup	120 grams
½ cup	60 grams

Nuts – Brazil nuts

1 cup	140 grams
½ cup	70 grams

Nuts – ground (almond)

1 cup	90 grams
¾ cup	70 grams
½ cup	45 grams

Chocolate – chips

1 cup	170 grams
½ cup	85 grams

Chocolate – grated

1 cup	70 grams
½ cup	35 grams

Sugar – granulated

1 cup	250 grams
½ cup	125 grams
¼ cup	65 grams
1 tablespoon	15 grams

Sugar – brown

1 cup	200 grams
½ cup	100 grams
¼ cup	50 grams

Sugar – icing

1 cup	130 grams
½ cup	65 grams
¼ cup	30 grams

Syrups – golden

1 cup	340 grams
½ cup	170 grams
¼ cup	85 grams

Syrups – maple and apple

1 cup	315 grams
½ cup	160 grams
¼ cup	80 grams

Honey

1 cup	350 grams
½ cup	175 grams
¼ cup	85 grams
1 tablespoon	25 grams

Yeast – active dry

1 tablespoon	10 grams
1 teaspoon	4 grams
¼ teaspoon	1 gram

Yeast – Surebake yeast mix

1 tablespoon	8 grams
1 teaspoon	3 grams

Dried mixed fruit – including chopped dried stone fruits sultanas and raisins

1 cup	140 grams
½ cup	70 grams
¼ cup	35 grams

Glacé cherries

1 cup	200 grams
½ cup	100 grams
¼ cup	50 grams

Glacé ginger

1 cup	150 grams
½ cup	75 grams

what went wrong?

The cake has sunk or the muffins have peaked or the mixture has curdled. Here's a basic guide to why.

Problem:

The creamed mixture has curdled

- The butter and sugar were not beaten until light and creamy. The butter should be much paler (light) in colour, almost cream colour when beaten correctly and the mixture should be thick. The butter needs to be soft (not cold or overly softened) and malleable to achieve this.
- Eggs were not at room temperature and/or they were not beaten in well enough after each addition.

Solution:

- Add a spoonful of the flour to bring the mixture back together and beat well, preferably at this point with an electric beater.

Problem:

The cake has sunk in the middle

- Too much raising agent (baking powder, whipped eggs, etc.), which causes the cake to rise too quickly and then collapse before it is firm enough to support its own structure.
- Too much sugar or too much flour.
- Cake tin too small or removed from the oven before the cake was cooked.

- Oven too high or the door was opened too early during the baking and the cold air caused the cake to collapse.

Solution:

- Cut the centre out of the cake, make into a ring cake and ice.
- Crumble the cooled cake and make truffles.
- Use to make trifle.

Problem:

Cake batter has overflowed during baking

- Too much raising agent.
- Tin too small. A mixture should come no higher up the cake tin than $2/3$ so that it has room to rise.

Solution:

- First clean the oven.
- Cut off any crusty pieces and decorate the cake. Cut the top of the cake level, if it has sunk, before decorating.

Problem:

Cake is too heavy

- Not enough raising agent (baking powder or whipped egg whites).
- Too much flour or over-mixing of the flour.
- Too heavy a hand when folding or mixing and the air has been knocked out.
- Too few eggs or maybe they were too small in size.
- Oven temperature too low.

Solution:

- Serve warm with custard as a pudding.
- Drench in syrup and serve with fruit and whipped cream.

Problem:

Bottom of the cake has burnt

- Thin tin or cake tin too dark.
- Cake baked too close to the bottom of the oven.

Solution:

- Trim away the dark base and ice.
- If the cake is dry as a result, drench with syrup.

Problem:

Top of the cake has burnt

- Cake was placed too high in the oven.
- Oven too hot.
- Cake cooked too long.
- Too much sugar in the recipe.

Solution:

- Trim off the top and turn upside down to decorate and serve.
- If the cake is dry as a result, drench with syrup.

Problem:

Fruit has sunk to the bottom

- Dried fruits that are coated in a sugar or sugar-like syrup can slip through soft cake mixtures to the bottom.

Solution:

- Once done there's very little you can do, but to prevent this rinse the fruit to remove the syrup and pat well dry on paper towel before using.

Problem:

Muffins or cake have peaked like Mt. Everest

- Batter was over-beaten.

Solution:

- Trim off the peak and ice the cake.
- Make muffins into butterfly cakes (see page 167).

emergency disguises

If something goes wrong, don't panic. If the family or guests are not told, they probably will never know. Try to resurrect failures as baking ingredients are expensive and it's also disheartening throwing good food out; try one of these ideas:

- If the cake is dry, pierce it all over with a skewer and spoon over a fruit or flavoured syrup, prepared from equal quantities of liquid and sugar, heated and stirred until the sugar dissolves. Or use the crumbs to make into truffles.

- If the cake breaks when coming out of a tin or when being handled, 'glue' the pieces together with icing and cover the cake with more icing or another topping.

- Crumbly biscuits can be used to make the base for a dessert, e.g. cheesecake.

- If the pavlova has over-browned and gone chewy, break it up and fold through whipped cream, yoghurt and fresh berries and pile into glasses for a summer meringue mousse.

basic pastry recipes

1¼ cups flour
½ teaspoon salt
125 grams chilled butter, diced
4–5 tablespoons ice-cold water

basic short pastry

makes 300 grams
(sufficient for a 23-cm flan tin)
preparation time **10 minutes**

Sift the flour and salt into a bowl. Using your fingertips, rub the butter into the flour until the mixture resembles fine crumbs.

Using a knife, stir in sufficient water until the pastry begins to form large clumps. When a small portion is gathered in the hand and pressed it should stay together.

Turn out onto a lightly floured bench and knead lightly to bring together. Do not over-knead as the pastry will become tough.

Wrap in greaseproof paper or plastic wrap and rest in the fridge for 30 minutes.

food processor method
Put the flour, salt and butter into a food processor fitted with the metal blade and process until the mixture resembles fine crumbs.

Pulse in sufficient water, until the mixture forms small moist balls of dough. Press a small amount of the dough balls together and if they form a mass sufficient water has been added.

Turn out onto a lightly floured bench and bring together. There is no need to knead pastry made in the food processor as this will have been done sufficiently by the processor. Wrap and rest in the fridge for 30 minutes.

where to use
🍃 For savoury tarts and pies.
🍃 For sweet tarts and tartlets where the filling is exceptionally sweet and a less-sweet pastry is required.

1½ cups flour
½ teaspoon salt
150 grams butter, chilled and
    diced
2 egg yolks
1–2 tablespoons chilled water

1½ cups flour
½ teaspoon salt
½ cup caster or icing sugar
4 egg yolks
100 grams butter, at room
    temperature

rich short pastry

makes 350 grams
(sufficient for a 23-cm flan tin)
preparation time 10 minutes

Sift flour and salt into a bowl. Using your fingertips, rub butter into flour until mixture resembles fine crumbs.

Using a knife, cut in egg yolks and sufficient water until pastry begins to form large clumps, which when gathered in the hand and pressed should stay together.

Turn the dough out and bring together. Wrap in greaseproof paper and refrigerate for 1 hour before using.

food processor method
Place the flour, salt and butter into a food processor fitted with the metal blade and process until the mixture resembles fine crumbs.

Pulse in the egg yolks and sufficient water, until the mixture forms small moist balls of dough. When a small portion is gathered in the hand and pressed it should stay together.

Turn out and bring together, kneading only lightly. Wrap in greaseproof paper and refrigerate for 1 hour.

where to use
‣ For richer style savoury tarts, quiches and pies.
‣ For sweet tarts and tartlets where the filling is exceptionally sweet and a buttery but not sweet pastry is preferred.

basic sweet short pastry

makes 350 grams
(sufficient for a 23-cm flan tin)
preparation time 10 minutes

Sift the flour and salt onto a bench and then make a well in the centre.

Place the sugar, egg yolks and butter into the centre and knead together using your fingertips, preferably of one hand only, as these are the coolest part of your hand.

Once the ingredients are well mixed, begin to bring in the flour from the edges. Continue using your fingertips.

Once all the flour is incorporated and the pastry is smooth, wrap in greaseproof paper or plastic wrap and refrigerate for 1 hour. This will allow the pastry to rest and makes it far more manageable when rolling out.

food processor method
Put the sugar, egg yolks and butter into the food processor fitted with a plastic or metal blade and process for 1 minute until light and creamy.

Pulse in the flour and salt until just mixed. Do not over-process.

Wrap in greaseproof paper or plastic wrap and refrigerate for 1 hour until required.

where to use
‣ Use for special sweet tarts, tartlets and flans.

basic icing recipes

1½ cups icing sugar
1 teaspoon butter, melted,
    optional
2–3 tablespoons warm water
    or milk

basic glacé icing

makes 1 cup
preparation time **5 minutes**

This is a basic, quick-to-make icing.

Sift the icing sugar into a bowl.

Add the melted butter and sufficient warm water or milk to make a smooth thick icing that can spread easily onto your baking.

variations

- **lemon**: Use the grated rind and juice of 1 lemon in place of the milk or water.
- **liqueur**: Use your favourite liqueur in place of the water.
- **mocha**: Dissolve 1 teaspoon coffee and 1 teaspoon cocoa in hot water before mixing with the remaining icing ingredients.
- **orange blossom**: Add 1–2 drops of orange blossom water to the icing.
- **orange**: Use the grated rind and juice of 1 small orange in place of the milk or water.
- **passion-fruit**: Add the grated rind of ½ lemon and the strained pulp of 1 passion-fruit to the icing. Add water if necessary. You can add the pips from the passion-fruit if wished.
- **peppermint**: Add peppermint essence to taste.
- **rosewater**: Add 1–2 drops of rosewater to the icing. Decorate the top of a cake with fresh rose petals.
- **simple chocolate**: Dissolve 1–2 tablespoons cocoa in the warm milk or water and allow to cool. Mix in the sifted icing sugar and sufficient extra milk or water to reach the desired consistency.
- **spice**: Add ½ teaspoon mixed spice to the icing sugar before sifting. Or use your favourite spice or a combination.

how to use

Glacé icing can be used to coat the top and sides of cakes, muffins, cup cakes, cream puffs, etc.

1 egg white (size no. 7)
about 2 cups icing sugar, sifted
1 teaspoon lemon juice

100 grams butter, at room
    temperature
1½ cups icing sugar
few drops vanilla essence
about 1–2 tablespoons milk

royal icing

makes ¾ cup
preparation time **15 minutes**

The hard icing is traditionally used for decorating wedding cakes, but can also be used to decorate cup cakes and used for piping where you want the piped name or greeting to become hard.

Place the egg white in a bowl and break up with a fork until it just begins to form bubbles of foam.

Using a wooden spoon, slowly begin to add a little icing sugar and lemon juice, stirring gently so as to incorporate as little air as possible.

Continue to add the icing sugar until the mixture is stiff and forms soft peaks. This is the ideal consistency for covering cakes. For piping, add additional icing sugar to make a very stiff icing.

Cover with a damp tea towel to prevent the icing forming a hard crust on top. If making ahead, cover the icing with plastic wrap or store in an airtight container. Stir gently before using.

basic butter icing

makes 1½ cups
preparation time **10 minutes**

This rich icing can also be used as a filling.

Beat the butter until it is pale and fluffy.

Sift the icing sugar and beat into the creamed butter with the vanilla essence and sufficient milk until you have a fluffy light mixture. If you need the mixture to spread more easily, then add a little more milk.

variations

- **almond**: Add 1 drop almond essence to the mixture and about ½ cup finely chopped toasted almonds.
- **chocolate**: Heat the 2 tablespoons milk and dissolve 2 tablespoons cocoa in it. Allow to cool before adding to the icing.
- **coffee**: Heat the 2 tablespoons milk and dissolve 1 tablespoon coffee in it. Allow to cool before adding to the icing.
- **lemon**: Add the grated rind of 1 lemon and use lemon juice in place of the milk.
- **mocha**: Heat the 2 tablespoons milk and dissolve 1 tablespoon cocoa and 1 teaspoon coffee in it. Allow to cool before adding to the icing.
- **orange**: Add the grated rind of 1 orange and use orange juice in place of the milk.
- **passion-fruit**: Add the pulp of 1 ripe passion-fruit.

150 grams dark chocolate
½ cup cream

125 grams dark chocolate,
    chopped
_25g_
_65g_

_25g_
50 grams butter, softened
2½ cups icing sugar
_325g_   _160g_
    _160g_

ganache or chocolate cream topping

makes ¾ cup
preparation time **10 minutes**

A rich chocolate glaze that's best used on rich chocolate cakes or cup cakes.

Place the chocolate and cream in a small jug or bowl and heat in the microwave on high power (100%) for about 1 minute. Stir and if the chocolate has not begun to melt, heat a further 30 seconds and stir again. Stir to make a smooth glaze.

Allow to cool before using.

rich chocolate icing

makes 2 cups
preparation time **10 minutes**

Melt the chocolate in a double saucepan or in the microwave. Cool.

Beat the butter until smooth. Beat in the cooled chocolate mixture and icing sugar.

100 grams white chocolate
2 tablespoons butter

1 cup icing sugar, sifted
about 2 tablespoons milk

1 egg yolk
2 tablespoons water

white chocolate icing

makes 1 cup
preparation time **5 minutes**

Melt the white chocolate and butter together. Stir in the icing sugar and sufficient milk to make a smooth, thick icing.

egg wash

makes 1 cup
preparation time **5 minutes**

For a rich glaze on pastry, biscuits, breads, use egg wash, also called egg glaze.

Beat the egg yolk and water together. Strain, if wished, through a small sieve. Keep covered.

From top to bottom:
white chocolate icing
royal icing
basic butter icing

biscuits

125 grams butter, softened
½ cup sugar
1 egg
1 tablespoon golden syrup or honey
1 tablespoon desiccated coconut,
    optional
1½ cups flour, sifted

basic biscuits

makes 24
preparation time **15 minutes**
cooking time **15 minutes**

This inexpensive basic biscuit recipe is ideal for children to learn simple baking techniques. From measuring, mixing, rolling, cutting out shapes, decorating, baking to even icing.

Preheat the oven to 180 °C. Lightly grease 1–2 baking trays or line with baking paper.

In a medium-sized bowl, beat butter, sugar, egg and golden syrup or honey together with a wooden spoon until creamy and light in colour.

Stir in the coconut, if using, and sifted flour. Mix only until combined.

Roll teaspoonfuls into balls and place on the prepared baking tray. Dip a fork in flour and shake off any excess. Press firmly onto each ball of biscuit dough to flatten gently. Alternatively, roll to a 3-mm thickness and cut into shapes.

Bake in the preheated oven for 15 minutes or until the biscuits begin to brown around the edges.

Transfer to a cake rack to cool. Keep in an airtight container.

variations
- Add ½–1 cup chocolate chips.
- Add the grated rind of 1–2 lemons or oranges.
- Roll mixture into balls and place on a greased tray. Press handle end of a wooden spoon into each ball and fill with jam or fruit mince.

250 grams butter, softened
1½ cups sugar
grated rind of 2 lemons
2 eggs
1 cup self-raising flour
1¼ cups flour
2 cups desiccated coconut

lemon biscuits

makes about 48
preparation time **15 minutes**
cooking time **12–15 minutes**

Tart, sweet and luscious – all in one delicious mouthful!

Preheat the oven to 180 °C. Lightly grease 1–2 baking trays or line with baking paper.

In a large bowl, beat the butter, sugar and lemon rind together well, until light and creamy. Add the eggs one at a time, beating well after each addition.

Sift the flours together and add to the creamed mixture with the coconut. Mix gently.

Place large teaspoonfuls of the mixture on the prepared trays and press down with the tines of a floured fork.

Bake in the preheated oven for 12–15 minutes until golden brown.

Transfer to a cake rack to cool. Once cold, store in an airtight container.

allyson's tip

Keep coconut in the freezer as like other nuts it will go rancid if kept in a warm kitchen cupboard.

Cookies are made of butter and love.
– Norwegian proverb

allyson's tip

To make chocolate Anzacs, melt 150 grams dark chocolate either in the microwave or over the top of a double saucepan. Dip half an Anzac into the melted chocolate and allow the excess to fall off. Place on a baking paper-lined tray and allow the chocolate to set before storing in an airtight container in a cool area.

1 cup flour
1 cup sugar
1 cup rolled oats
1 cup desiccated coconut
175 grams butter

2 tablespoons golden syrup
1 teaspoon vanilla essence
1 teaspoon baking soda
2 tablespoons boiling water

anzac biscuits

makes about 36
preparation time **15 minutes**
cooking time **12–15 minutes**

My Dad was a 'Digger' and proud of it – and the one thing that best recalls that time when we all pulled together is the Anzac biscuit, created with love by mums and daughters to send to their sons and fathers at the Front.

Preheat the oven to 180 °C. Lightly grease 1–2 baking trays or line with baking paper.

In a large bowl, sift flour with a good pinch of salt. Stir in the sugar, rolled oats and coconut and make a well in the centre.

In a saucepan, melt the butter, golden syrup and vanilla essence together.

Dissolve the baking soda in the boiling water. Mix into the melted butter and quickly pour into the well. Mix all ingredients together quickly.

Roll tablespoonfuls of the mixture into balls and place on the prepared trays. Flatten with the tines of a floured fork.

Bake in the preheated oven for 12–15 minutes until the biscuits have flattened out and have become a reddish-brown colour.

Transfer to a cake rack. They will crispen as they cool. Once cold, store in an airtight container.

275 grams butter, softened
½ cup icing sugar
1 teaspoon vanilla essence
1½ cups pure flour
½ cup cornflour
1 quantity lemon butter icing
    (see page 29)

125 grams butter, softened
½ cup sugar (caster is good)
1 egg
grated rind of 1 lemon
1 cup flour
1 cup cornflour

1 teaspoon baking powder
1 teaspoon ground mace or
    nutmeg
½ cup raspberry jam
icing sugar to dust

melting moments

makes about 24
preparation time 10 minutes
cooking time 18–20 minutes

It is the lemon butter icing that really makes these delicious morsels the mouth-watering sensation we've come to know and love.

Preheat the oven to 160 °C. Lightly grease 1–2 baking trays or line with baking paper.

Beat the butter, icing sugar and vanilla essence together until light and creamy.

Sift together the flour and cornflour and mix into the creamed mixture. Do not over-mix.

Roll teaspoonfuls into balls and place on the prepared baking tray.

Dip a fork into flour and shake off the excess. Flatten the dough balls gently by pressing with the tines of the fork. Dip the fork into the flour as needed.

Bake in the preheated oven for 18–20 minutes until the biscuits are firm and beginning to brown a little around the edges.

Transfer to a cake rack to cool. Once cold, join with the lemon butter icing.

raspberry kisses

makes 18–20
preparation time 15 minutes
cooking time 12–15 minutes

I have wonderful, fond memories of a house full of baking aromas and these were one of my mother's all-time favourites.

Preheat the oven to 180 °C. Lightly grease 1–2 baking trays or line with baking paper.

In a large bowl, beat the butter and sugar together until creamy.

Add the egg and lemon rind and beat well.

Sift together the flours, baking powder and mace or nutmeg and stir into the creamed mixture. Do not over-mix or the cookies will be tough.

Place mounded teaspoonfuls of mixture onto the prepared baking trays.

Bake in the preheated oven for 12–15 minutes until the cookies firm up and have begun to brown lightly around the edges.

Transfer to a cake rack to cool. Once cold, join two similar-shaped cookies together with raspberry jam and dust lightly with icing sugar. Store in an airtight container.

allyson's tips

raspberry kisses

❧ Mace is the lacy outside covering of the nutmeg that when fresh is a deep fire-engine red. Once dried it becomes a deep ochre-orange colour.

❧ The flavour of mace is more delicate than nutmeg, but both can easily be interchanged.

L–R:
yo-yos (page 42)
raspberry kisses
melting moments

250 grams butter, softened
½ cup icing sugar
1¾ cups pure flour
½ cup custard powder

custard-flavoured butter icing
1 quantity butter icing
   (see page 29)
2 tablespoons custard powder

200 grams butter, softened
¼ cup caster sugar
1 egg yolk
½ teaspoon vanilla essence
3 tablespoons brandy
½ teaspoon ground cardamom
¼ cup flaked almonds, finely
   chopped
1½ cups flour
½ teaspoon baking powder
1 tablespoon rosewater
¾ cup icing sugar

yo-yos

makes 24
preparation time **15 minutes**
cooking time **12–15 minutes**

Press mixture through a biscuit forcer to make a delightful shape.

Preheat the oven to 180 °C. Lightly grease 1–2 baking trays or line with baking paper.

In a medium-sized bowl, beat the butter and icing sugar together until light and creamy.

Sift the flour and custard powder together and gently mix into the creamed ingredients. Do not over-mix as the biscuits will be tough.

Roll teaspoonfuls into balls and place on the prepared trays. Dip the tines of a fork into flour and shake off any excess. Press the fork into the balls of dough lightly to flatten a little.

Bake in the preheated oven for 12–15 minutes until the edges are just beginning to turn a pale brown. Cool on a cake rack.

When cold, join two similar-sized cookies together with the custard-flavoured butter icing.

custard-flavoured butter icing
Beat the butter icing and custard powder together well.

Pictured on previous page.

greek shortbread cookies

makes 36–40
preparation time **20 minutes**
cooking time **20–25 minutes**

Deliciously spiked with cardamom and rosewater, serve these cookies blanketed in icing sugar with freshly brewed coffee, scented with a cardamom pod or two.

Preheat the oven to 160 °C. Lightly grease 1–2 baking trays or line with baking paper.

Beat the butter and sugar together until light and fluffy. Beat in the egg yolk, vanilla, 1 tablespoon of the brandy, cardamom and almonds.

Sift the flour and baking powder together and stir into the creamed mixture to form a soft, manageable dough.

Taking 1 tablespoon of dough at a time, roll out on a lightly floured surface to make a thick oval, about 5–6 cm long and 2–3 cm wide. Place on the prepared trays and pinch the ends to make a crescent shape. Repeat with the remaining mixture.

Bake in the preheated oven for 20–25 minutes until pale, golden and firm. Allow to stand for 5–10 minutes.

Mix the rosewater and remaining brandy together and use a pastry brush to brush each biscuit lightly while they are still warm. Dust generously with icing sugar.

Transfer to a cake rack to cool. Store in an airtight container.

did you know?

A horseshoe or crescent shape symbolises good luck.

greek shortbread cookies

L–R:
gingernuts
ginger crispies

2 cups flour
1 cup caster sugar
2 teaspoons ground ginger
1 teaspoon ground cinnamon
½ teaspoon baking soda

125 grams butter, grated or diced
1 egg
2 teaspoons golden syrup or treacle

125 grams butter, softened
½ cup sugar
1 egg
1¾ cups self-raising flour, sifted

1 cup finely chopped crystallised ginger
1 cup Cornflakes, crushed

gingernuts

makes about 40
preparation time 20 minutes
cooking time 12–15 minutes

Local legend suggests John Griffin was the first to commercially make gingernuts sometime in the 1890s. These seriously crisp biscuits are ideal for dunking.

Preheat the oven to 160 °C. Lightly grease 1–2 baking trays or line with baking paper.

In a medium-sized bowl, sift the flour, sugar, ginger, cinnamon and baking soda together.

Using fingertips, rub the butter into the dry ingredients until the mixture resembles fine breadcrumbs. Make a well in the centre.

Beat the egg with the golden syrup or treacle, and add to the dry ingredients. Work into a firm dough using your hands. If necessary, add 1 tablespoon of water to the mixture.

Roll teaspoonfuls into balls and place on the prepared oven tray.

Bake in the preheated oven for 12–15 minutes until the biscuits are golden and firm to the touch.

Transfer to a cake rack to cool. Store in an airtight container.

ginger crispies

makes 30
preparation time 15 minutes
cooking time 15–20 minutes

Cereals are a regular ingredient in most family homes, making them ideal to use in simple baking recipes like this.

Preheat the oven to 180 °C. Lightly grease 1–2 baking trays or line with baking paper.

In a medium-sized bowl, beat the butter and sugar together until light and creamy.

Add the egg and beat well.

Stir in the sifted flour and ginger.

Roll teaspoonfuls into balls. Roll each ball firmly into the crushed Cornflakes pressing the Cornflakes onto the dough. Place on the prepared trays. Dip the tines of a fork into flour and shake off any excess. Press the fork into the balls of dough lightly to flatten.

Bake in the preheated oven for 15–20 minutes until firm and golden. Leave on the tray for 1 minute before transferring to a cake rack to cool. These ginger crispies will crispen as they cool.

1 cup desiccated coconut
½ cup sugar
1 tablespoon cornflour
1 egg, beaten
16 whole, or 8 halved, glacé cherries

coconut macaroons

makes 16
preparation time 10 minutes
cooking time 15 minutes

Simple and easy for children to make, these macaroons were a favourite in my childhood.

Preheat the oven to 180 °C. Lightly grease 1–2 baking trays and dust with a light covering of cornflour. Alternatively, line with baking paper.

In a medium-sized bowl, mix together the coconut, sugar and cornflour and make a well in the centre.

Add the beaten egg and mix with a knife to form a moist mass.

Place heaped dessertspoons of mixture onto the prepared trays. Top with a whole or halved glacé cherry.

Bake in the preheated oven for 15 minutes or until lightly golden.

Transfer while warm to a cake rack to cool. Store in an airtight container.

Grandmothers never run out of hugs or cookies

- Author Unknown

175 grams butter, softened
¾ cup brown sugar
¾ cup sugar (caster is good)
2 eggs
2¼ cups flour
1 teaspoon baking powder
2 cups chocolate chips

toll house chocolate chip biscuits

makes about 30
preparation time **15 minutes**
cooking time **20 minutes**

Toll House biscuits are said to have been created by a Mrs Ruth Wakefield, manager of the Toll House restaurant in Massachusetts. She apparently added chocolate bits to her basic biscuit recipe, so creating every child's favourite chocolate chip biscuit!

Preheat the oven to 180 °C. Lightly grease 1–2 baking trays or line with baking paper.

In a large bowl, beat the butter and sugars together until very light and creamy.

Add the eggs one at a time, beating well after each addition.

Sift the flour and baking powder together over the creamed mixture. Sprinkle over the chocolate chips and stir together gently.

Use an ice-cream scoop to scoop the mixture onto the prepared trays, leaving plenty of room for the biscuits to spread.

Bake in the preheated oven for 20 minutes or until the biscuits are beginning to brown lightly around the edges and are firm to the touch.

Transfer to a cake rack to cool. Store in an airtight container.

variations
- Add the grated rind of 1 orange for jaffa toll house biscuits.
- Use half and half white chocolate and dark chocolate chips.
- Substitute 1 cup of flour with 1 cup of wholemeal flour.

250 grams butter, softened
1 cup icing sugar, sifted
grated rind of 1 orange
1–2 teaspoons orange blossom water
2½ cups flour, sifted
70-gram packet blanched whole
    almonds or pine nuts

did you know?

Orange blossom water is prepared from a distillation of the orange flowers (blossom) of bitter orange trees such as the Seville orange. The oil (neroli) that rises to the top is removed leaving the fragrant water to be bottled, usually in dark coloured bottles to avoid flavour damage caused by bright sunlight.

orange blossom water butter biscuits

makes 30
preparation time **15 minutes**
cooking time **12–15 minutes**

These rich buttery biscuits are scented with highly fragrant orange blossom water and are delicious enjoyed on their own, or served with fresh fruit salads or poached fruits, especially apricots.

Preheat the oven to 180 °C. Lightly grease 1–2 baking trays or line with baking paper.

Beat the butter and sugar together until very light and fluffy. Beat in the orange rind and orange blossom water.

Gently mix in the flour to make a firm biscuit dough.

Roll teaspoonfuls into balls and place on the prepared trays.

Dust the palm of your hand with flour and shake off any excess. Flatten the biscuits lightly with the palm of your hand.

Arrange an almond, or several pine nuts in the shape of a flower, on top of each biscuit.

Bake in the preheated oven for 12–15 minutes, or until the biscuits are beginning to colour around the edges.

Remove to a cake rack to cool. Store in an airtight container.

250 grams butter, diced
¾ cup sugar
1 egg
few drops almond essence
2 cups flour
1 teaspoon baking powder
35–40 whole blanched almonds

brown butter biscuits

makes 35–40
preparation time **15 minutes**
cooking time **15–20 minutes**

Why brown butter? The secret to a biscuit full of flavour is to use salted butter and to allow the butter to become nut brown in colour when melted.

Preheat the oven to 160 °C. Lightly grease 1–2 baking trays or line with baking paper.

Put the butter into a saucepan and melt over a moderate heat until it has turned a nut-brown colour. Remove immediately and stand on a damp cloth to stop any further cooking. Scrape any sediment from the base of the saucepan into the butter.

When cool, use a wooden spoon to beat in the sugar, egg and almond essence.

Sift the flour and baking powder together and stir into the butter.

Roll heaped teaspoonfuls of the mixture into balls and place on the prepared baking trays.

Flatten with your fore and middle fingers and place an almond into the centre of each biscuit.

Bake in the preheated oven for 15–20 minutes until lightly golden.

Cool on a cake rack. Once cold, store in an airtight container.

L–R:
chocolate orange swirls
chocolate button biscuits

allyson's tips

chocolate orange swirls

❧ Melting chocolate in the microwave is easier than over a pot of simmering water. Times will vary depending on the wattage of the microwave. Be careful not to over-cook as chocolate burns quickly and leaves an acrid odour in the microwave.

❧ If you do not have a piping bag, roll teaspoonfuls of the dough into balls, place on a baking tray, press down with the tines of a fork and bake.

allyson's tips

chocolate button biscuits

❧ If you do not have 2 egg yolks, use 1 egg.

❧ Use cooking or compound chocolate buttons for this recipe. These products have been designed not to melt under heat and remain relatively the same shape when baked.

did you know?

❧ We know jaffa as a name for foods with a combination of orange and chocolate. The name comes from Jaffa in Israel, an historic port city from where locally grown oranges were exported.

300 grams butter, softened
1 cup icing sugar
grated rind of 2 oranges
1 egg
2½ cups flour
½ cup cocoa

chocolate coating
100 grams dark chocolate, roughly chopped
1 teaspoon Kremelta

1 tablespoon instant coffee granules
1 tablespoon boiling water
1 teaspoon vanilla essence
250 grams butter, softened
1 cup sugar (caster sugar is best)

2 egg yolks
2½ cups flour
2 teaspoons baking powder
50 dark chocolate buttons

chocolate orange swirls

makes 40
preparation time 10 minutes
cooking time 12–15 minutes

Morning coffee will never be the same. Orange and chocolate are an irresistible combination.

Preheat the oven to 180 °C. Lightly grease 1–2 baking trays or line with baking paper.

Beat the butter, icing sugar and orange rind together until light and creamy. Add the egg and beat well.

Sift the flour and cocoa together and stir into the creamed mixture. Do not over-mix as the biscuits will become tough when baked.

Put the mixture into a piping bag fitted with a large star nozzle and pipe medium-sized rosettes onto the prepared trays.

Bake in the preheated oven for 12–15 minutes. Cool on a cake rack.

chocolate coating

Melt the chocolate and Kremelta in a small bowl in the microwave on high power (100%) for 1 minute, stir and if necessary, microwave a further 15–30 seconds. Stir well. Spread the melted chocolate on the base of each biscuit and allow to set. Alternatively, pipe ribbons of chocolate over the top of each biscuit. Once the chocolate has set, store the biscuits in an airtight container.

chocolate button biscuits

makes 50
preparation time 10 minutes
cooking time 20 minutes

These crunchy morsels are an ideal way to use up egg yolks left over from making meringues or pavlovas.

Preheat the oven to 160 °C. Grease 1–2 baking trays well or line with baking paper.

Dissolve the coffee granules in the boiling water and vanilla essence, set aside to cool.

Beat the butter and sugar together until light and creamy. Beat in the egg yolks and dissolved coffee mix.

Sift the flour and baking powder together and stir into the creamed mixture. Do not over-mix.

Roll teaspoonfuls of the mixture into even-shaped balls and place on the prepared baking trays.

Press a chocolate button firmly onto the top of each one.

Bake in the preheated oven for 20 minutes.

Cool on the trays for 1 minute before transferring to cake racks to cool thoroughly. Store in an airtight container.

200 grams butter, softened
¾ cup firmly packed brown sugar
1 egg
1–2 teaspoons vanilla essence
1¾ cups flour
¼ cup cocoa
2 teaspoons baking powder
½ cup dessicated coconut
2 cups Cornflakes

chocolate icing
1½ cups icing sugar
2 tablespoons cocoa
1 teaspoon butter, melted
2–3 tablespoons warm milk or water

afghans

makes 24
preparation time **15 minutes**
cooking time **15–18 minutes**

These Kiwi favourite cookies can be made with almost any breakfast cereal, making them a great tin-filler.

Preheat the oven to 180 °C. Lightly grease 1–2 baking trays or line with baking paper.

In a large bowl, beat the butter and sugar until light and creamy.

Beat in the egg and vanilla essence.

Sift together the flour, cocoa and baking powder over the creamed ingredients and scatter the coconut and Cornflakes on top. Mix all the ingredients together. Do not over-mix or the Cornflakes will become too finely crushed.

Spoon large tablespoonfuls of the mixture onto the prepared trays.

Bake in the preheated oven for 15–18 minutes.

Cool on a cake rack before icing with chocolate icing.

Store in an airtight container.

chocolate icing

In a bowl, sift icing sugar and cocoa. Blend in melted butter and warm milk or water until you have a thick icing of spreadable consistency.

allyson's tips

- If you do not have any Cornflakes on hand substitute crushed Weet-Bix or a similar style of breakfast cereal.

- The finest flavoured cocoa powders are those with the higher percentage of cocoa solids. To check this, read the ingredient label where the percentage will be stated.

- Do not substitute cocoa powder with drinking chocolate, the two are not interchangeable.

- The flavour of cocoa in baked goods is almost always enhanced with the addition of vanilla essence.

250 grams butter, diced
1 cup caster sugar
¼ cup golden syrup
1 tablespoon honey
¾ cup flaked almonds
½ teaspoon cinnamon

2 teaspoons ground cardamom
1 teaspoon ground ginger
1 teaspoon baking soda
1 tablespoon water
3–3½ cups flour

fondant icing
300 grams store-bought
　fondant
2 tablespoons caster sugar
2 tablespoons boiling water
1 teaspoon glucose

christmas
spice cookies

makes 40 biscuits
preparation time **4 hours 20 minutes** (includes chilling)
cooking time **12–15 minutes**

These are a traditional Scandinavian Christmas cookie, which are usually prepared in hand-carved wooden biscuit moulds. For simplicity, I have rolled the dough out, cut festive shapes and decorated with an easy fondant icing. These are special enough to be given as a gift at Christmas or hung on the tree for decoration.

In a saucepan, melt together the butter, sugar, golden syrup, honey, almonds, cinnamon, cardamom and ginger, stirring gently over a moderate heat.

Bring to the boil and then remove from the heat.

Dissolve the baking soda in the water then stir into the warm butter mixture. Cool for 5 minutes.

Sift 3 cups of the flour into a large bowl and make a well in the centre.

Pour in the warm butter mixture and, using a wooden spoon, mix to a stiff dough. Add more flour if necessary to achieve this. Turn out onto a floured bench and knead lightly.

Divide the mixture in half and wrap in plastic wrap or greased paper and refrigerate for 4 hours or until firm. This makes the mixture easier to roll out.

Preheat the oven to 180 °C. Lightly grease 2–3 baking trays.

On a lightly floured bench, roll the mixture out to 3-mm thickness. Cut into shapes and place on the prepared trays.

Bake in the preheated oven for 12–15 minutes or until deep golden brown, but not burnt.

Transfer to a cake rack to cool. Store in an airtight container and decorate as wished. These biscuits will keep for 3–4 weeks if kept in a sealed container.

fondant icing
Cover the fondant with hot water from the tap and set aside for 10 minutes or until the fondant has begun to soften. Pour off the water.

Dissolve the sugar in the boiling water and add to the fondant with the glucose. Warm in the microwave for 1–2 minutes or until the fondant has begun to soften, stir to make a smooth icing. Cover with plastic wrap and allow to cool.

To decorate, spread the spice biscuits with the fondant and decorate with sliver cachous or other edible decorations.

250 grams butter, softened
½ cup icing sugar
1 egg
1 tablespoon rosewater
2 cups rice flour
1½ teaspoons baking powder
2 teaspoons ground cardamom

rosewater butter icing
1 quantity butter icing (see page 29)
few drops rosewater

(see page 29)

allyson's tip

Rosewater is made from distilled fragrant rose petals, and as it is very strong in flavour, it should be used with a gentle hand.

persian rice cookies

makes 40
preparation time **15 minutes**
cooking time **20 minutes**

Known in Persia (Iran) as 'nan berinji', these heavenly shortbread-like biscuits are made with rice flour, and are flavoured with cardamom – a very special spice.

Preheat the oven to 180 °C. Lightly grease 1–2 baking trays or line with baking paper.

Beat the butter and icing sugar together until very light and creamy. Add the egg and rosewater and beat well.

Sift the rice flour, baking powder and cardamom together and sprinkle evenly over the top of the creamed mixture. Stir in with a large spoon.

Roll teaspoonfuls of the mixture into balls and place on the prepared trays. Press down with the tines of a fork. Alternatively, the mixture is ideal to use in a biscuit forcer (press).

Bake in the preheated oven for 20 minutes until the cookies have begun to brown very lightly around the edges.

Carefully transfer to a cake rack to cool. Store in an airtight container.

If wished, join two biscuits together with the rosewater butter icing.

rosewater butter icing
Beat the butter icing with the a few drops of rosewater to flavour.

100 grams butter, softened
⅓ cup sugar
¼ cup milk
1 cup flour
1 cup wheat bran
3 teaspoons baking powder

bran biscuits

makes about 36
preparation time **15 minutes**
cooking time **18–20 minutes**

These biscuits are unbelievably moreish. This recipes comes from my mentor Tui Flower, who almost always has them on hand. They are best served lightly buttered.

Preheat the oven to 180 °C. Lightly grease 1–2 baking trays or line with baking paper.

Beat butter, sugar and milk together until well mixed.

Stir in the flour, bran and baking powder to make a soft mix.

Turn the dough out onto a heavily floured surface and bring together. You may need to add more flour.

Roll out to 2-mm thickness. Cut into shapes and place on the prepared trays.

Bake in the preheated oven for 18–20 minutes or until crispy and brown.

Transfer to a cake rack to cool. Store in an airtight container.

1 cup whole unblanched
    almonds
125 grams butter, softened
¾ cup sugar
1 tablespoon almond liqueur
2 eggs
2 cups flour
1½ teaspoons baking powder

¾ cup almonds, toasted
¾ cup Brazil nuts, toasted
¾ cup pistachio nuts
125 grams butter, softened
¾ cup caster sugar
2 teaspoons almond essence
2 eggs
2 cups flour
1½ teaspoons baking powder
1 cup finely diced glacé papaya
1 cup finely diced dried
    pineapple
½ cup diced red glacé cherries
¼ cup diced glacé angelica or
    green glacé cherries
½ cup ground almonds

almond biscotti

makes about 60
preparation time 20 minutes
cooking time 45 minutes

Preheat the oven to 180 °C. Lightly grease 1–2 baking trays or line with baking paper.

Place the almonds on a tray or in a cake tin and roast in the preheated oven for about 10 minutes until they smell nutty and are slightly browned. Cool before chopping into chunky pieces. Reduce the oven to 160 °C.

Beat the butter, sugar and liqueur together until light and creamy. Add the eggs one at a time.

Sift together the flour and baking powder and stir into the creamed mixture with the almonds. Turn onto a lightly floured surface and divide the mixture in half.

Roll each portion into a sausage shape about 3 cm in diameter. Place on the prepared trays.

Bake in the preheated oven for 25 minutes, or until the rolls are set and lightly browned on top.

Transfer the rolls to a cake rack and leave to cool for 10 minutes. Slice the rolls diagonally into 1-cm wide slices and place the slices back on the tray.

Return to the oven for a further 10 minutes, turning over after 5 minutes. They should be slightly toasted in colour. Cool on a cake rack. Store in an airtight container.

christmas biscotti

makes 40–50 slices
preparation time 20 minutes
cooking time 40 minutes

These biscotti remind me of a church's stained glass windows.

Preheat the oven to 160 °C. Lightly grease 1–2 baking trays or line with baking paper.

Chop the nuts into chunky pieces.

In a large bowl, beat butter, sugar and almond essence together until very creamy. Add the eggs one at a time.

Sift the flour and baking powder together and stir into the creamed mixture with the nuts, fruit and almonds.

Turn the dough out onto a lightly floured bench and divide in half. Roll each portion out into a sausage shape to about 3 cm in diameter. Place on the prepared tray.

Bake in the preheated oven for 25–30 minutes until the rolls are lightly browned and firm to the touch.

Remove from the oven and allow the rolls to cool on a cake rack for 10–15 minutes.

Using a bread knife, slice the biscotti diagonally into ½-cm wide slices. Place the slices on the baking tray and return to the oven for a further 7–8 minutes until lightly toasted. Cool the biscotti on a cake rack and keep in an airtight container.

did you know?

❧ Biscotti is an Italian word that means to cook twice. Tradition has it that these molar-testing biscuits, which are ideal dipped into a hot coffee or red wine, originated in Tuscany, Northern Italy.

❧ Glacé angelica is the preserved stem of *Angelica*, an archangelic plant. Grown in cooler climates, crystallising the stems takes much time, hence its expense. The finished emerald green colour is enhanced by dying as during the sugar saturation process the stems become a dull green.

L–R:
almond biscotti
strawberry liqueur biscotti (page 66)
christmas biscotti

¾ cup crystallised or dried
  strawberries
¼ cup strawberry eau de vie or
  berry fruit juice
¾ cup whole unblanched
  almonds, toasted
125 grams butter, softened

¾ cup sugar
2 eggs
2¼ cups flour
1 teaspoon baking powder
½ teaspoon baking soda

strawberry
liqueur biscotti

makes 48–54
preparation time **30 minutes**
cooking time **45 minutes**

**Dunk these tasty morsels in white wine or have them
with coffee. You can easily vary them with the
different crystallised or dried summer fruits.**

Preheat the oven to 160 °C. Lightly grease 1–2 baking
trays or line with baking paper.

Cut the strawberries in half. In a small saucepan, bring
the strawberry eau de vie or berry fruit juice to scalding
point. Add the strawberries and set aside for 10 minutes
or until cool.

Chop the almonds into small chunky pieces.

In a large bowl, beat the butter and sugar together
until creamy.

Add the eggs one at a time, beating well after each
addition until the mixture is smooth.

Sift the flour, baking powder and baking soda together
and stir into the creamed mixture with the almonds,
strawberries and soaking liquid. Stir only until combined.

Turn onto a lightly floured bench. Divide the mixture in
half and roll each portion out to a sausage about 3 cm in
diameter and the length of the baking tray.

Place on the prepared trays about 5 cm apart. Gently
flatten the top of both rolls.

Bake in the preheated oven for 30 minutes or until they
are lightly browned and firm to the touch.

Cool the rolls on a cake rack for 10 minutes then slice
them diagonally into ½-cm wide slices.

Place the slices back on the tray and return the biscotti
to the oven for a further 7– 8 minutes until lightly
coloured. Turn them over and cook a further 5 minutes.

Cool on a cake rack. Store in an airtight container.

Pictured on previous page.

125 grams butter, chilled and
   diced
125 grams Cheddar or Edam
   cheese, grated
125 grams flour
1 teaspoon curry powder,
   optional
toppings: sesame seeds, poppy
   seeds, finely chopped nuts
   of your choice

savoury
cheese biscuits

makes 30
preparation time 10 minutes
cooking time 12–15 minutes

The simplest recipe for these moreish cheesy biscuits uses equal quantities by weight of flour, butter and grated tasty Cheddar. Throw everything in the food processor for a very delicious nibble in minutes.

Preheat the oven to 200 °C. Line 1–2 baking trays with baking paper.

Put the butter, cheese, flour and curry powder, if using, into a food processor and process until the mixture forms a stiff ball of dough.

Turn out onto a lightly floured bench and roll the dough out to ½-cm thickness.

Cut into 4–5-cm rounds or your preferred shapes.

Place on the prepared trays and sprinkle with one of the selected toppings.

Bake in the preheated oven for 12–15 minutes or until golden and crisp.

Cool one minute before transferring carefully onto a cake rack to cool completely.

Store in an airtight container. Freeze when cold, if wished.

variations
- Use ½ wholemeal and ½ plain flour.
- Use half Cheddar or Edam and half blue cheese.

Pictured overleaf.

4 cups fine oatmeal or oat
    flakes
1 teaspoon baking powder
½ teaspoon salt
75 grams butter, melted
1¼ cups boiling water

3½ cups flour
40-gram packet poppy seeds
½ teaspoon salt
75 grams butter, chilled and
    diced
1 cup cold milk

traditional oatcakes

makes 30
preparation time **15 minutes**
cooking time **15–20 minutes**

Oatcakes are delicious served with almost any cheese.

Preheat the oven to 190 °C. Grease 1–2 baking trays well or line with baking paper.

Put the oatmeal or oat flakes, baking powder and salt into a food processor and pulse to mix.

Turn the food processor on. Pour the butter and water down the feed tube until it is absorbed.

Knead lightly on a bench dusted with a little oatmeal or flour. Roll out as thinly as possible. If the edges break, pinch them together.

Cut into 6–7-cm rounds and transfer to the prepared trays. Use a slide as the oatcakes are very delicate.

Bake in the preheated oven for 15–20 minutes or until the oatcakes are a pale fawn shade.

Cool on a cake rack. Store in an airtight container.

variations
- Add 1 tablespoon finely chopped fresh rosemary or thyme, great with blue cheese.
- Add 1 tablespoon dried chilli flakes, great with creamy-style cheeses.
- Add 2 teaspoons celery seeds, ideal with Cheddar.

poppy seed crackers

makes 48
preparation time **20 minutes**
cooking time **10–12 minutes**

Freshly baked home-made crackers are a delight to serve with your favourite soft-style cheese.

Preheat the oven to 190 °C. Lightly grease 1–2 baking trays or line with baking paper.

Put the flour, poppy seeds and salt into a food processor and pulse only to sift. Add the butter and process until the mixture resembles fine breadcrumbs.

With the motor running, pour the milk down the feed tube as fast as the flour can absorb it. Process 1 minute.

Bring the dough together on a lightly floured surface. Cover with plastic wrap and leave to rest for 10–15 minutes. This results in dough that's easier to roll out and biscuits that are tender when baked.

On the lightly floured surface, roll the dough out as thinly as possible. If rolling becomes hard, cover with a clean tea towel or plastic wrap and allow the dough 10 more minutes' resting time.

Cut 5–6-cm rounds and place on the prepared trays. Prick each biscuit thoroughly with the tines of a fork. Bake in the preheated oven for 10–12 minutes until the biscuits are lightly golden. Cool the biscuits on a cake rack. Store in an airtight container.

allyson's tip

If you cannot find oatmeal, process 4½ cups rolled oats in a food processor until finely milled. This will equate to 4 cups once processed.

did you know?

In times past, oatcakes were buried in a meal chest, containing oatmeal. These 'cakes' were the staple food of the Scots for centuries, as oats were the only cereal that would grow in the weather.

Back L–R:
traditional oatcakes
savoury cheese biscuits (page 67)
Front:
poppy seed crackers

shortbread

allyson's tip

rose petal shortbread

You can make the shortbread in a food processor though the butter and sugar cream will not be as light. However, it is twice as quick and the end product is still good. Pulse in the flour and petals, so as not to cut the petals to shreds.

did you know?

Rosewater is prepared from distilling fragrant rose petals. It is an essential flavouring in Turkish delight, halva and baklava. A small bottle will last for years if kept out of direct sunlight.

250 grams butter, softened
¾ cup caster or icing sugar
1–2 drops rosewater, optional
2 cups flour
½ cup cornflour
½ cup fresh baby rose petals

rose petal shortbread

makes 36 pieces
preparation time **15 minutes**
cooking time **30–35 minutes**

Baby rose petals turn a basic shortbread into something special. I prefer pale pink petals as red petals turn brownish when cooked.

Preheat the oven to 160 °C. Lightly grease 1–2 baking trays or line with baking paper.

In a large bowl, beat together the butter, sugar and rosewater, if using, until light and fluffy and pale in colour.

Sift the flours and stir into the creamed mixture with the rose petals.

Turn out onto a lightly floured bench, bring together and knead lightly. Roll out to 5-mm thickness. Cut into shapes such as hearts.

Place the shortbreads onto the prepared trays and use the tines of a fork to mark each shortbread three times or use a small cutter to mark heart shapes. Refrigerate for 10 minutes or up to 2 hours.

Bake in the preheated oven for 30–35 minutes until they are light brown in colour. If you like your shortbread a little darker, cook a further 5 minutes.

Cool on the tray for 10 minutes before transferring to a cake rack. Once cold, store in an airtight container.

200 grams butter, softened
½ cup caster sugar
2 cups flour, sifted
¼ cup rice flour, sifted

scottish shortbread

makes 24–30 pieces
preparation time **15 minutes**
cooking time **50–60 minutes**

Adding rice flour gives this shortbread a soft, delicate texture. Use cornflour if you do not have rice flour.

Preheat the oven to 160 °C. Grease and line a 20-cm x 30-cm slice tin with baking paper.

Beat the butter and sugar together well until light and creamy.

Work the flours into the creamed mixture. Do not over-mix.

Press the mixture into the prepared slice tin.

Use a small knife to mark into 24–30 squares or bars and mark each piece three times with the tines of a fork.

Bake in the preheated oven for 50–60 minutes or until a sandy brown colour.

Cool in the tin for 10 minutes then turn out onto a board and cut into pieces using the lines already marked on the shortbread.

Cool on a cake rack. Store in an airtight container.

Pictured overleaf.

250 grams butter, softened
¾ cup caster sugar
1 teaspoon vanilla essence
2 cups flour, sifted
½ cup semolina
1 cup very coarsely chopped
    dark and/or milk chocolate
2 tablespoons caster sugar for
    sprinkling on top

1 cup flour
¾ cup caster sugar
1 cup whole unblanched
    almonds
100 grams butter, melted
1 teaspoon almond essence

ballindoch shortbread

makes 24–30 pieces
preparation time 20 minutes
cooking time 45 minutes

This delicious shortbread recipe originates from the Castle Ballindoch at Inverness in Scotland and I love the texture the semolina gives the shortbread and the indulgence of loads of chocolate.

Preheat the oven to 160 °C. Grease and line a standard 20-cm x 30-cm Swiss roll tin with baking paper.

Beat the butter, sugar and vanilla essence together until the mixture is pale in colour and fluffy in texture.

Stir in the sifted flour, semolina and chocolate.

Press the mixture firmly into the prepared slice tin.

Mark the dough into 24–30 pieces without cutting all the way through the shortbread. Sprinkle evenly with the extra sugar.

Bake in the preheated oven for 45 minutes or until golden and the shortbread is firm to the touch.

Remove from the oven and stand 10 minutes before cutting through the shortbread where you have marked it into pieces.

Leave in the tin to cool completely before storing in an airtight container.

almond shortbread

makes 20 pieces
preparation time 15 minutes
cooking time 20 minutes

This new and improved version of an old classic is not so much a shortbread, as a slice, but the broken pieces are rich and buttery.

Preheat the oven to 160 °C. Grease and line a standard 20-cm x 30-cm Swiss roll tin with baking paper.

Put the flour, caster sugar and almonds into a food processor. Pulse to coarsely chop the almonds and mix ingredients together.

Pulse the melted butter and almond essence down the feed tube as fast as the dry ingredients can absorb it.

Once all the butter and essence has been added, pulse until the mixture resembles coarse crumbs in texture.

Press the mixture into the prepared tin.

Bake in the preheated oven for 20 minutes or until the shortbread begins to brown.

Cool in the tin. Break into odd-shaped pieces to serve. Store in an airtight container.

variation

❧ Use ½ cup pistachio nuts in place of the almonds and add the grated rind of 1 lemon.

allyson's tips

ballindoch shortbread
Avoid using white chocolate in this recipe as it over-cooks.

almond shortbread
1 cup whole almonds is approximately 90–100 grams.

did you know?

Traditional shortbread in Scotland is associated with the Yule season. This includes Christmas and New Year. The round shortbread cakes that are notched around the edges symbolise the sun's rays.

From Top:
ballindoch shortbread
scottish shortbread (page 73)
almond shortbread

125 grams caster or icing sugar
250 grams butter, softened
375 grams flour, sifted

150 grams butter, softened
¼ cup caster or icing sugar
1 egg yolk
1½ cups flour, sifted
2 tablespoons rice flour or
    cornflour, sifted
12–15 glacé cherries, halved

aunt jean's shortbread

makes 24–30 pieces
preparation time 15 minutes
cooking time 25–30 minutes

This is my Aunt Jean's shortbread recipe. A classic that's worth keeping on hand.

Preheat the oven to 160 °C. Lightly grease 1–2 baking trays or line with baking paper.

Beat the sugar and butter together until very pale and creamy in colour. It should be a whipped cream colour and the sugar, if using caster, dissolved.

Sift the flour carefully onto the creamed mixture and work in by hand or with a wooden spoon.

Place the mixture into the fridge for about 1 hour or until it is firm enough to handle. Turn out onto a floured surface and knead lightly.

Roll the dough out to a 1-cm thickness and cut into circles or shapes. Place on the prepared trays and mark the tops with the tines of a fork.

Bake in the preheated oven for 25–30 minutes or until firm and lightly golden – certainly not brown. Cool on a wire rack and store in an airtight container.

These taste best once they have had time to allow the flavours to marry (about 7 days).

mrs beeton's shortbread

makes 24–30 pieces
preparation time 15 minutes
cooking time 25–30 minutes

An old recipe from the second edition of *Mrs Beeton's Book of Household Management* from the 1860s. This shortbread is not at all sweet, reflecting the change over time for sweeter-style baking.

Preheat the oven to 160 °C. Lightly grease 1–2 baking trays or line with baking paper.

In a medium-sized bowl, beat the butter, sugar and egg yolk until creamy and well beaten.

Work the flours into the creamed mixture. Turn out onto a very lightly floured surface and form into a mass.

Roll out to 0.5–0.7-cm thickness. Cut into shapes and place on the prepared trays. Decorate each biscuit with a cherry half.

Bake in the preheated oven for 25–30 minutes until lightly golden around the edges.

Cool on a cake rack before storing in an airtight container.

allyson's tips

aunt jean's shortbread

🌾 To cut time, roll the prepared dough into a 3-cm sausage-shaped cylinder. Refrigerate for 1 hour. Cut 1-cm rounds and place on the baking tray.

🌾 The mixture can also be frozen at this point. Cut into slices, reassemble the log and then roll it in baking paper. Place in an airtight bag and freeze. That way you can break off and bake as many biscuits as you want at any one time. Bake from frozen, allowing an extra 8–10 minutes' cooking time.

mrs beeton's shortbread

🌾 Do not over-knead the mix as this will produce a tough shortbread.

🌾 The addition of an egg adds richness and was predominantly done in Ayrshire, southwest Scotland.

L–R:
aunt jean's shortbread
caramel shortbread (page 78)
mrs beeton's shortbread

250 grams butter
½ cup firmly packed soft brown
    sugar
1¾ cups flour, sifted
½ cup cornflour, sifted

caramel shortbread

makes 24–30 pieces
preparation time 15 minutes
cooking time 35–40 minutes

Brown sugar brings a caramel-like flavour to shortbread.

Preheat the oven to 160 °C. Lightly grease 1–2 baking trays or line with baking paper.

In a medium-sized bowl, beat the butter and sugar together until pale and well whipped in texture.

Work the flours into the creamed mixture. Do not over-process. Turn the mixture out onto a floured surface and bring together.

Roll the dough out to 1-cm thickness and cut into squares or rounds. Place on the prepared baking tray. Mark with the tines of a fork.

Bake in the preheated oven for 35–40 minutes until firm to the touch.

Allow to cool on the tray for 10 minutes before transferring to a cake rack to cool. Store in an airtight container.

Pictured on previous page.

200 grams butter, softened
½ cup caster sugar
grated orange rind of 2 oranges
2 cups flour, sifted
½ cup desiccated coconut

summer citrus shortbread

makes about 60 small or 30 larger shapes
preparation time 15 minutes
cooking time 15 minutes

I enjoy these best in summer. The crisp texture is an ideal partner to poached fruits or enjoyed with a late afternoon cup of tea.

Preheat the oven to 180 °C. Lightly grease 1–2 baking trays or line with baking paper.

In a medium-sized bowl, beat the butter, sugar and orange rind together until light and creamy.

Work the flour and the coconut into the creamed mixture.

Turn the dough out onto a floured surface and bring together. Do not over-work the dough.

Roll the dough out to 0.3-cm thickness and cut into shapes. Place on the prepared baking tray.

Bake in the preheated oven for 15 minutes or until lightly golden and firm.

Cool on the tray for 10 minutes before transferring to a cake rack to cool. Store in an airtight container.

allyson's tip

summer citrus shortbread
This recipe can be quickly prepared in the food processor. Once the butter, sugar and orange rind have been processed, pulse the flour and coconut to avoid over-processing the coconut.

Shortbread is an ideal recipe to mark children's names in:

Pat a cake, pat a cake, baker's man,
Bake me a cake as fast as you can;
Pat it, prick it and mark it with 'B',
And put it in the oven for Baby and me.

summer citrus shortbread

Mary, Mary quite contrary,
how does your garden grow?
With silver bells and cockle shells
and pretty maids all in a row.

2½ cups flour, sifted
½ cup caster sugar
2 teaspoons caraway seeds
175 grams butter, melted
¼ cup tepid milk

queen mary's petticoat tailles

makes 9
preparation time **15 minutes**
cooking time **25 minutes**

A favourite, it is said, of Mary, Queen of Scots. Caraway with its warm, sweet, biting taste, brightened baking in centuries past. Caraway is thought to be the oldest cultivated spice in Europe.

Preheat the oven to 180 °C. Lightly grease a baking tray or line with baking paper.

In a large bowl, stir together the sifted flour, caster sugar and caraway seeds. Make a well in the centre.

Using a knife, stir in the melted butter and milk to make a heavy dough.

Turn out onto a lightly floured surface and knead lightly. The texture will be almost rubbery – quite different from other shortbreads in this book.

Mould into a round and then carefully roll out to around 0.5-cm thick. Transfer to the prepared tray.

Cut into a perfect round shape, about 26-cm in diameter, using a dinner plate inverted on top as a guide. Use a small sharp knife to trim away any excess.

Using the forefinger of one hand and the forefinger and thumb on the other, pinch the edge all the way around.

Use an 8–10-cm round cutter to cut a circle out of the centre (an upturned glass is fine).

Mark the wheel of shortbread in 8 even pieces with a knife, but do not cut all the way through. Place the circle on the tray.

Bake in the preheated oven for 25 minutes until golden around the edges.

Cool on the tray for 10 minutes before cutting into pieces, where marked.

Transfer to a cake rack to cool. Store in an airtight container.

slices & brownies

Who was Louise?

While I have never been able to truly confirm who Louise was, it seems likely that she was Princess Louise, the fourth daughter of Queen Victoria. About this time (mid to late 1800s) baking and the ritual of taking afternoon tea was at its height. Many baked foods, including puddings, were named for a visit by a member of the royal family or a birth or marriage.

louise slice

100 grams butter, softened
1 cup caster sugar
3 eggs, separated
2 tablespoons milk
1 teaspoon vanilla essence

2 cups self-raising flour
½ cup red jam (raspberry, plum or currant)
¾ cup desiccated coconut

175 grams butter, melted
½ teaspoon vanilla essence
1¼ cups flour
½ teaspoon baking powder
¾ cup brown sugar
1¼ cups rolled oats

chocolate & walnut filling
75 grams butter, melted
1 cup caster sugar
¼ cup cocoa

2 eggs, beaten
½ teaspoon vanilla essence
1¾ cups flour
½ teaspoon baking powder
¾ cup chopped walnuts
½ cup milk
1 quantity chocolate butter icing (see page 29)

louise slice

makes **30 pieces**
preparation time **20 minutes**
cooking time **25–30 minutes**

The ultimate tin-filler – loved by Kiwis of all ages.

Preheat the oven to 180 °C. Grease and line a standard 24-cm x 30-cm Swiss roll tin.

Beat together the butter, ¼ cup caster sugar, egg yolks, milk and vanilla essence until well mixed. Gently stir in the flour.

Spread the mixture into the prepared tin. Spread the jam evenly over the base.

In a clean bowl, whisk the egg whites until stiff but not dry. Beat in the remaining caster sugar until the mixture is thick and glossy. Fold in the coconut and spread over the slice.

Bake in the preheated oven for 25–30 minutes. Cool in the tin before removing to a board to slice into squares. Store in an airtight container.

chocolate walnut squares

makes **36–40 pieces**
preparation time **30 minutes**
cooking time **30 minutes**

Preheat the oven to 180 °C. Grease and line a large 24-cm x 30-cm slice tin.

Mix butter and vanilla essence together and cool.

Sift the flour and baking powder into a bowl. Stir in sugar and oats and make a well in the centre. Pour the butter into the well and mix together. Scatter the base evenly over the prepared tin and press down firmly.

Bake in the preheated oven for 10 minutes. While the base is cooking, prepare the filling.

chocolate & walnut filling

In a bowl, stir together the butter, caster sugar and cocoa. Add the eggs and vanilla essence and mix well. Sift flour and baking powder together and stir gently into the liquid ingredients with the walnuts and milk. Spread the filling evenly over the hot base.

Return to the oven for a further 20 minutes or until the filling is cooked and firm to the touch. Cool in the tin for 10 minutes before transferring to a cake rack.

Ice with chocolate butter icing when cold and cut into squares to serve. Store in an airtight container.

Pictured overleaf

allyson's tips

🍂 Cocoa will vary greatly in quality depending on the brand bought. Should you need to, add 2–3 tablespoons more cocoa, don't forget to take out the same quantity of flour – otherwise the mixture will be dry.

🍂 Baking tins are much easier to clean if washed as soon as possible after the baking. Dry in the oven to ensure they are not stored damp and rust or go mouldy.

🍂 Never scratch tins to remove stubborn remains as the cake or slice will stick next time.

L–R:
chocolate rough slice
chocolate mint slice
chocolate walnut squares (page 85)

1¼ cups self-raising flour, sifted
1½ cups desiccated coconut
1 cup sugar
¼ cup finely chopped chocolate
    or chocolate hail
¼ cup cocoa
200 grams butter, melted

1½ cups flour
¼ cup cocoa powder
1½ cups brown sugar
1 cup desiccated coconut
3 cups Cornflakes or lightly
    crushed Weet-Bix
250 grams butter, melted
1 teaspoon vanilla essence
extra desiccated coconut, to
    decorate

1 quantity peppermint icing
    (see page 28)
1 quantity simple chocolate
    icing (see page 28)

chocolate rough slice

makes 30 pieces
preparation time 15 minutes
cooking time 15–20 minutes

The children will be fighting over the spoon when they tackle this easy one-bowl recipe.

Preheat the oven to 180 °C. Grease and line a large 24-cm x 30-cm slice tin.

In a large bowl, stir together the flour, coconut, sugar, chocolate and cocoa and make a well in the centre. Pour in the melted butter and mix together.

Press into the prepared tin.

Bake in the preheated oven for 15–20 minutes until firm.

Allow to cool in the tin before icing. Cut into slices or squares and store in an airtight container.

Ice with simple chocolate icing (see page 28) or chocolate butter icing (see page 29), if wished.

chocolate mint slice

makes 40 pieces
preparation time 15 minutes
cooking time 25 minutes

A favourite recipe from school days. If peppermint is not to your liking, just ice with your favourite icing.

Preheat the oven to 180 °C. Grease and line a large 24-cm x 30-cm slice tin.

Sift flour and cocoa powder into a bowl. Stir in brown sugar, coconut, Cornflakes or Weet-Bix. Make a well in the centre.

Stir butter and vanilla essence into dry ingredients and mix well. Press mixture firmly into prepared tin.

Bake in the preheated oven for 25 minutes or until the top of the slice is firm to the touch.

Cool for 10 minutes before spreading the peppermint icing evenly over the warm slice. Refrigerate until cold.

Carefully spread the chocolate icing on top of the peppermint icing and sprinkle with a little extra coconut to decorate, if wished. Cut into squares and keep in an airtight container.

2 cups flour
1 teaspoon baking powder
½ teaspoon salt
¾ cup caster sugar
1 cup finely chopped
    crystallised ginger

250 grams butter, softened
1 egg, beaten
1–2 tablespoons extra caster
    sugar

125 grams butter, softened
¾ cup caster sugar
1 tablespoon golden syrup
few drops lemon essence or
    grated rind of 1 lemon
2 eggs

2 cups flour
2 teaspoons baking powder
1 cup currants
2 tablespoons milk
1 quantity basic butter icing
    (see page 29)

ginger slice

makes **16** pieces
preparation time **15 minutes**
cooking time **40 minutes**

This recipe is a favourite from a special uncle who ran a small restaurant in the village town of Beauty Point on the Tamar river in northern Tasmania, way back in the '70s.

Preheat the oven to 180 °C. Grease and flour the base of a 23-cm round cake or flan tin.

Sift the flour, baking powder, salt and sugar into a bowl. Stir in ¾ of the ginger and make a well in the centre.

Add the softened butter and beaten egg into the well and, using a wooden spoon, combine the mixture to form a soft dough.

Use floured hands to press into the prepared tin, making dimples with fingertips. Sprinkle the remaining ginger and extra caster sugar on top.

Bake in the preheated oven for 40 minutes. Cool in the tin for 10 minutes before turning out onto a cake rack to cool thoroughly. Serve in wedges.

Store in an airtight container. The flavour improves on keeping.

albert squares

makes **20** pieces
preparation time **15 minutes**
cooking time **35 minutes**

Currants are often forgotten in favour of other trendier dried fruits, but they're an economical and delicious dried fruit to keep on hand for baking.

Preheat the oven to 160 °C. Grease and line a standard 20-cm x 30-cm Swiss roll tin.

In a large bowl, beat the butter, sugar, golden syrup and lemon essence or grated lemon rind together with a wooden spoon until light and creamy.

Add the eggs one at a time, beating well after each addition.

Sift the flour and baking powder together and stir into the creamed mixture with the currants and milk.

Spread into the prepared tin.

Bake in the preheated oven for 35 minutes until cooked.

Cool in the tin for 10 minutes before transferring to a cake rack to cool.

Spread with butter icing when cold and cut into squares. Store in an airtight container.

allyson's tips

ginger slice
When recipes call for softened butter, the butter should be very soft – but not melted. Once melted, butter changes from a solid fat to an oil and will not perform as intended in the recipe.

albert squares
Always store dried fruits in a container with a loose-fitting lid where the air can circulate to prevent moulding and a stale taste being imparted.

L–R:
albert squares
eltham slice (at rear, page 90)
ginger slice

100 grams butter
¾ cup sugar
1 tablespoon golden syrup
½ teaspoon vanilla essence
1 egg, beaten

1 cup flour
1 teaspoon baking powder
1 cup desiccated coconut
1 cup mixed dried fruit
icing sugar, to dust

1½ cups flour
½ cup icing sugar
¼ cup cocoa
100 grams butter, diced
1 egg
3–4 tablespoons cold water
500 grams dark chocolate,
    chopped

50 grams Kremelta
180-gram packet
    marshmallows, chopped
1½ cups dried cranberries
¾ cup raw pistachio nuts

eltham slice

makes **30 pieces**
preparation time **20 minutes**
cooking time **25–30 minutes**

**A favourite from my days as an exchange student to
Eltham, Taranaki.**

Preheat the oven to 160 °C. Grease and line the base of
a standard 20-cm x 30-cm Swiss roll tin.

In a saucepan, melt together the butter, sugar, golden
syrup and vanilla essence. Cool.

Add the egg to the cooled mixture and beat well. (If the
mixture is hot, the egg will cook like scrambled egg.)

Sift the flour and baking powder together and stir into
the saucepan with the coconut and mixed fruit. Spread
into the prepared tin.

Bake in the preheated oven for 25–30 minutes until cooked.

Stand in the tin for 10 minutes before turning out onto
a cake rack to cool. Dust with icing sugar and cut into
slices or squares. Store in an airtight container.

variations
- Add 1 teaspoon grated orange rind.
- Use brown sugar for a more caramel-like flavour.
- Use treacle in place of golden syrup.

Pictured on previous page.

pistachio & cranberry rocky road

makes **30 pieces**
preparation time **30 minutes**
cooking time **10–12 minutes**

**Look for flavoured cranberries for added taste –
often they can be purchased with a blueberry or
raspberry flavour.**

Preheat the oven to 180 °C. Grease and line a standard
20-cm x 30-cm Swiss roll tin.

Place the flour, icing sugar and cocoa in a bowl. Lightly
rub the butter into the dry ingredients.

Beat the egg and water together and mix into the dry
ingredients to make a pliable dough.

Press into the prepared tin using a floured glass to help
roll the dough out evenly in the slice tin.

Bake in the preheated oven for 10–12 minutes or until
the pastry is cooked. Cool the pastry in the tin.

Put chocolate and Kremelta into a microwave-proof
bowl and heat on high power (100%) for 2–3 minutes
or until chocolate is almost melted. Stir until smooth.

Scatter the marshmallows, cranberries and pistachio
nuts over the base and pour over the melted chocolate.
Tap the tin on a bench to even out the ingredients.

Refrigerate for 1–2 hours or until set. Use a hot knife to
cut into small pieces. Store in the refrigerator.

pistachio & cranberry rocky road

Oranges and lemons, say the bells of St. Clement's,
You owe me five farthings, say the bells of St. Martin's.

1¼ cups flour
½ teaspoon baking powder
125 grams butter, chilled
¼ cup caster sugar
grated rind of 1 lemon

lemon topping
3 eggs, at room temperature
1 cup caster sugar
grated rind of 2 lemons
juice of 3 lemons (about ½ cup)
¼ cup flour, sifted

divine lemon squares

makes about **20 pieces**
preparation time **20 minutes**
cooking time **40 minutes**

These are SO moreish with the crispy base and squidgy lemon topping, once tried they'll become a firm favourite to have with friends!

Preheat the oven to 180 °C. Grease and line a standard 20-cm x 30-cm Swiss roll tin.

Put the flour, baking powder, butter, sugar and lemon rind into a food processor and process until the mixture forms soft beads of dough. Turn into the prepared tin and press firmly into the base. Even out by rolling a floured glass over the base.

Bake in the preheated oven for 12–15 minutes or until lightly golden. While cooking, prepare the topping.

Lemon topping
Using an electric beater beat the eggs and caster sugar together until light and fluffy. Fold in the grated lemon rind, lemon juice and flour.

Pour topping over the hot base.

Return to the oven for a further 25 minutes until the topping is spongy, golden and cooked.

Allow to cool in the tin. Dust with icing sugar before serving. Use a hot knife to cut into squares.

caramel filling
390-gram can condensed milk
50 grams butter
2 tablespoons golden syrup

base
175 grams butter, softened
¼ cup sugar
1 teaspoon vanilla essence
1½ cups flour, sifted
½ cup rolled oats

caramel oat slice

makes 40 pieces
preparation time 20 minutes
cooking time 30–35 minutes

As a young home economist, I worked on a delightful baking book for Nestlé and this pretty classic recipe is still one of my favourites.

Prepare the filling. Put the condensed milk, butter and golden syrup into a small saucepan and stir over a low heat for 4–5 minutes until the mixture becomes thick and golden. Cool.

Preheat the oven to 180 °C. Grease and line the base of a square 23-cm x 23-cm slice or cake tin with baking paper.

In a large bowl, beat the butter, sugar and vanilla together until light and creamy.

Stir the flour into the creamed mixture with the oats and work in the dry ingredients to make a moist crumbly mixture.

Press about ¾ of the mixture over the base of the prepared tin.

Pour over the cooled caramel filling and spread out evenly. Scatter over the remaining crumble mixture.

Bake in the preheated oven for 30–35 minutes until golden.

Cool in the tin for 10–15 minutes before transferring to a cake rack to cool. As the slice is very rich, cut into small squares to serve.

Store in an airtight container.

1 cup sugar
2½ cups desiccated coconut
2½ cups rolled oats
250 grams butter, melted

allyson's tips

❧ Use standard rolled oats for this recipe, the thick wholegrain oats are too large and the finished result will be crumbly.

❧ Once opened keep oats in the fridge.

did you know?

❧ Rolled oats were developed by the Quaker Oat Company in America in 1877. They are rolled and steamed before drying. This process lessens the cooking time of oats considerably.

flapjacks

makes 30 pieces
preparation time 15 minutes
cooking time 25–30 minutes

Oaty and buttery, these squares are scrumptious!

Place the oven rack in the lower section of the oven. Preheat the oven to 160 °C. Grease and line the base and sides of a standard 20-cm x 30-cm Swiss roll tin.

In a large bowl, stir together the sugar, coconut and rolled oats and make a well in the centre.

Pour in the melted butter and stir well to mix the butter evenly through the dry ingredients.

Press into the prepared tin.

Bake in the preheated oven for 25–30 minutes or until well browned.

Use a small sharp knife to cut into squares or triangles while warm but leave to cool completely in the tin.

Once cold, cut along marked lines and store in an airtight container.

rich brownie.

250 grams dark chocolate, chopped
250 grams butter, diced
4 eggs
1½ tablespoons vanilla essence
2 cups caster sugar
3 tablespoons instant coffee granules
1 cup flour, sifted
1 cup coarsely chopped walnuts

rich brownie

makes 40 pieces
preparation time 25 minutes
cooking time 40 minutes

Preheat the oven to 180 °C. Grease and line the base and sides of a 25-cm square cake tin.

Melt the chocolate and butter in the top of a double boiler, stirring occasionally just until the mixture is smooth. Allow to cool.

In a large bowl, beat the eggs, vanilla essence, caster sugar and instant coffee granules together with an electric beater until the mixture is light and very voluminous.

Fold in the melted chocolate mixture, flour and walnuts.

Pour the mixture into the prepared cake tin.

Bake in the preheated oven for 35 minutes. The batter will be a little uncooked in the centre.

Cool to room temperature and then place the tin into the refrigerator overnight.

Lift the brownies out and cut into squares. The brownies will have a crispy crust on them. Serve dusted with icing sugar or topped with chocolate butter icing (see page 29).

250 grams quality white chocolate, roughly chopped
250 grams butter, diced
1 cup caster sugar
4 eggs
1 tablespoon vanilla essence
2 cups flour, sifted
1 cup pistachio nuts or pecans, chopped
1 quantity white chocolate icing (see page 30)

white chocolate brownie

makes about 24–30 pieces
preparation time 30 minutes
cooking time 30–35 minutes

Preheat the oven to 160 °C. Grease and line the base and sides of a large 25-cm square cake tin.

Place chocolate and butter in the top of a double saucepan and heat over boiling water until just melted. Alternatively, microwave on high power (100%) for about 2 minutes. Be careful not to over-cook the chocolate as it will burn easily. Stir until smooth and leave to cool.

Using an electric mixer, beat the sugar, eggs and vanilla essence together until the mixture is thick and fluffy.

Sift the flour over the beaten egg mixture and fold in alternately with the cooled chocolate mixture. This is easiest done with a slotted spoon. Fold in the pistachio nuts or pecans. Turn the mixture into the prepared cake tin.

Bake in the preheated oven for 30–35 minutes until the top is lightly golden but the centre is still a little soft.

Remove from the oven and cool to room temperature. Refrigerate for 3–4 hours. Remove from the tin, ice with the white chocolate icing and decorate with pistachio nuts or as wished.

Pictured overleaf.

allyson's tips

⤷ Use a damp knife when cutting brownies. Wipe the blade clean of any moist brownie mixture with each cut.

⤷ For even-size pieces, mark brownies or slices with a ruler before cutting.

vanilla brownie
⤷ For a richer butterscotch flavour use ½ soft brown sugar, ½ muscovado sugar.

L–R:
vanilla brownie
family brownie
white chocolate brownie (page 99)

100 grams butter, softened
1¼ cups brown sugar
1 tablespoon golden syrup
1 tablespoon vanilla essence
2 eggs

1 cup flour, sifted
½ cup walnuts, chopped
1 quantity coffee butter icing
  (see page 29)
½ cup walnut halves, optional

150 grams milk or dark
  chocolate, chopped
150 grams butter, softened
1 cup caster sugar
2 eggs
1 teaspoon vanilla essence

¾ cup flour, sifted
2 tablespoons cocoa
½ cup hazelnuts, pecans
  or walnuts, toasted and
  chopped
¼ cup milk

vanilla brownie

makes 16 pieces
preparation time 20 minutes
cooking time 30–35 minutes

A delightful twist on a classic. Add a handful of white chocolate drops if wished. The vanilla and brown sugar create a delicious butterscotch flavour.

Preheat the oven to 180 °C. Grease and line the base and sides of a 23-cm square cake tin.

In a large bowl, beat together the butter, brown sugar, golden syrup and vanilla essence until creamy and fluffy.

Add the eggs one at a time, beating well after each addition.

Fold the flour into the creamed mixture with the chopped walnuts.

Turn the batter into the prepared cake tin.

Bake in the preheated oven for 30–35 minutes or until a skewer inserted comes out clean.

Allow the brownie to cool in the tin for 20 minutes before turning out. Ice with coffee butter icing and decorate with walnuts, if wished. Cut into small squares to serve. Keep refrigerated.

family brownie

makes 20 pieces
preparation time 30 minutes
cooking time 30–40 minutes

This squidgy brownie is quick to make and ideal for the family. It's not too rich, yet has plenty of chocolate flavour.

Preheat the oven to 160°C. Grease and line a 20-cm square cake tin.

Heat the chocolate in the microwave on high power (100%) for 1½ minutes or until melted. Cool.

Beat the butter and sugar until very light and creamy. Add the eggs one at a time, beating well after each addition. Beat in the cooled chocolate and vanilla.

Carefully fold in the sifted flour and cocoa and the nuts alternately with the milk.

Transfer the batter into the prepared cake tin.

Bake in the preheated oven for 30–40 minutes until a skewer inserted into the centre of the brownie comes out almost clean. The centre should still be a little cakey.

Cool in the tin on a cake rack for 1 hour before turning out and cutting into squares. Dust with icing sugar, if wished. Keep in an airtight container.

scones, pikelets & pancakes

2 cups flour
4 teaspoons baking powder
½ teaspoon salt
50 grams butter, chilled
¾–1 cup milk

basic scones

makes 16–20
preparation time **10 minutes**
cooking time **10–12 minutes**

Fresh scones are perennial favourites as they are easy to make and take only a few basic ingredients. Create your own touches from this basic recipe.

Place the oven rack towards the top of the oven. Preheat the oven to 230 °C. Grease a baking tray or line with baking paper.

Sift the flour, baking powder and salt into a large bowl.

Dice the butter and rub into the dry ingredients until the mixture resembles fine crumbs. Make a well in the centre.

Pour in sufficient milk and mix quickly with a knife to make a soft dough. Knead very lightly on a bench dusted with flour.

Roll or press out to 2-cm thickness.

Cut into 3-cm rounds or squares and place on the prepared tray. Brush with milk or egg wash to glaze.

Bake in the preheated oven for 10–12 minutes until well risen, golden and cooked.

Transfer to a clean tea-towel-covered cake rack. Cover the top of the scones with the tea towel and serve hot or warm.

variations

- Date & orange scones – Add 2 tablespoons sugar to the flour. Once the butter is rubbed in, stir through ½ cup chopped dried dates and the grated rind of 1 orange. Use the juice from the orange if wished, making up with milk to the measure required. Sprinkle with sugar after glazing and before baking.
- Cheese scones – Add ½ cup grated cheese and 2 tablespoons finely chopped fresh parsley, chives or thyme to the flour once the butter is rubbed in. Once cut and on the tray, brush with milk and sprinkle a little extra grated Cheddar-style cheese on top of each scone.
- Spicy pinwheels – Add 2 tablespoons sugar to the flour. Complete the recipe. Roll the dough out to a 20-cm x 30-cm rectangle. Brush the dough with melted butter and sprinkle over 2–3 tablespoons brown sugar and 1–2 teaspoons mixed spice. Roll up from the long side and cut into 12 even rounds.
- Vary flours, and grains too, for texture and taste. Substitute ¼ cup oat bran for ¼ cup flour. For wholemeal scones substitute 1 cup wholemeal flour for 1 cup flour.

allyson's tips

➳ If there's only self-raising flour in the house, use that making sure the baking powder is omitted.

➳ For a richer scone add 1 egg with about ¾ cup milk for the dough.

L–R:
date & orange scones
cheese scones
spicy pinwheels

There are few hours in life more agreeable than the hour dedicated to the ceremony known as afternoon tea.

– Henry James (1843–1916), American author

2 cups self-raising flour
¾ cup lemonade
½ cup cream

waiheke lemonade scones

makes 8 wedges
preparation time **10 minutes**
cooking time **15–20 minutes**

Quick to make, these scones are ideal made into a round and served as a wedge with your favourite jam or spread.

Set the oven rack towards the top of the oven. Preheat the oven to 220 °C. Grease a baking tray or line with baking paper.

Sift the flour into a bowl and make a well in the centre.

Pour the lemonade and cream into the centre and use a knife to mix together to make a soft dough.

Turn out onto a lightly floured surface and knead very lightly.

Pat into an 18–20-cm round and place on the prepared tray. Brush with milk to glaze.

Use a sharp cook's knife to mark the scone into 8 even wedges without cutting all the way through.

Bake in the preheated oven for 15–20 minutes or until cooked. Transfer to a clean tea-towel-covered cake rack to cool. Serve warm.

scone etiquette
- Scones should never be cut in half, they only need a knife inserted and then they are torn into two halves.
- Devonshire tea is the name given to scones, warmed and served with clotted cream and jam.
- On a tiered cake rack, scones should always be in the middle, the sandwiches on the bottom and the sweet cakes on the top.

2–3 rashers rindless bacon, diced
1½ cups self-raising flour
¼ teaspoon baking soda
1 cup soft mashed potato, cooled
100 grams feta, crumbled

2 tablespoons chopped fresh parsley
1 egg, lightly beaten
¼ cup milk
2–3 tablespoons grated Parmesan
  or Cheddar-style cheese

potato, bacon & feta scones

makes 12–16
preparation time **10 minutes**
cooking time **12–15 minutes**

Make a change from brunch pancakes to these tasty savoury scones.

Set the oven rack towards the top of the oven. Preheat the oven to 220 °C. Grease a baking tray or line with baking paper.

Pan fry the bacon until crisp. Cool.

Sift the flour and baking soda together into a bowl. Use a knife to gently mix through the potato, feta, bacon and parsley and make a well in the centre.

Beat the egg and milk together and pour into the well. Use a knife to mix to a soft dough. Add more milk if necessary (the amount of milk required depends on the softness of the mashed potato).

Turn the dough onto a lightly floured surface. Knead very lightly until smooth, roll or pat out to about 2.5–3-cm thickness and cut into 4-cm circles, squares or triangles.

Place the scones close together on the prepared baking tray. Brush with a little milk and sprinkle with the cheese.

Bake in the preheated oven for 12–15 minutes until well risen and golden brown and cooked. Transfer to a clean tea-towel-covered cake rack to cool. Serve warm.

2½ cups self-raising flour
1 teaspoon baking powder
½ teaspoon salt
½ cup oat bran
50 grams butter, chilled
1¼ cups milk

annie's oat bran scones

makes 16
preparation time **10 minutes**
cooking time **10–12** minutes

The oat bran gives these scones a sweet nutty flavour – delicious with jam and cream or cheese. Best, though, is toasted the next day and served hot buttered.

Place the oven rack towards the top of the oven. Preheat the oven to 220 °C. Grease a baking tray or line with baking paper.

Sift together the self-raising flour, baking powder and salt. Stir in the oat bran.

Dice the butter and rub into the flour mixture with your fingertips until it resembles breadcrumbs. Make a well in the centre.

Pour the milk into the well and mix with a knife to form a soft dough.

Turn out onto a lightly floured surface, knead gently and press or roll out into a large 3-cm thick square.

Cut the dough into 16 squares and transfer to the prepared tray, placing the scones close together. Brush with milk to glaze.

Bake in the preheated oven for 10–12 minutes or until golden and cooked.

Transfer to a clean tea-towel-covered cake rack. Cover the top of the scones with the tea towel. Serve warm with butter or your favourite jam.

allyson's tip

Use your fingertips when rubbing the butter into the dry ingredients as fingertips are the coolest part of the hand. Using palms (which are warm) will make the butter greasy.

did you know?

The origin of the word scone is thought to be Scottish, from their word for flour 'sconbrot'.

In Scotland and northern England it is pronounced *skon*, but in London and south it is *skoan*.

2 cups self-raising flour
2 tablespoons sugar
¾ cup milk
1 egg, beaten
75 grams butter, melted

cinnamon topping
3 tablespoons flour
3 tablespoons sugar
1 teaspoon ground cinnamon
50 grams butter, melted

cinnamon scone tea ring

serves 6–8
preparation time **15 minutes**
cooking time **30 minutes**

This 'more dash than cash' variation on a quick and simple scone recipe is ideal for a girls' morning tea.

Preheat the oven to 200 °C. Grease a 20-cm ring tin well.

Sift the flour into a bowl and stir through the sugar. Make a well in the centre.

Beat the milk and egg together and pour into the well. Use a knife to mix quickly into a soft dough with the butter. Spread the thick batter evenly around the centre of the prepared ring tin.

cinnamon topping
Stir the flour, sugar, cinnamon and butter together. Scatter the cinnamon topping over the dough.

Bake in the preheated oven for 30 minutes. Allow to stand in the tin for 5 minutes before serving in slices from the tin.

variations
- Add the grated rind of 1 lemon or orange to the scone dough.
- Use demerara sugar for a crunchier topping.

25 grams butter
1 cup gluten-free flour
1½ teaspoons gluten-free baking
    powder
¼ cup sugar

2–4 tablespoons currants
½ cup milk
1 egg
grated rind of 1 lemon

gluten-free lemon & currant pikelets

makes 12
preparation time **5 minutes**
cooking time **10 minutes**

Adding a little browned butter to this recipe adds a nice sweet nutty flavour. For honey-lovers, use half sugar and half manuka or rewa rewa honey.

Melt the butter in a frying pan and cook until nut brown. Remove from the heat.

Sift the flour, baking powder and sugar into a bowl. Stir in the currants and make a well in the centre.

Beat together the milk, egg and lemon rind and pour into the well. Stir together with a wooden spoon, adding the browned butter at the end.

Place dessertspoonfuls of the batter in a lightly greased frying pan over a medium heat for about 1 minute. Once bubbles appear on the surface and burst, turn the pikelets over to cook a further minute or so until well-browned and cooked. Place on a cake rack while cooking the remaining batter mixture.

Serve the pikelets warm with softened butter or lemon curd.

50 grams butter
1 cup self-raising flour
¼ cup sugar
1 egg
¾ cup milk

basic pikelets

makes 12
preparation time **5 minutes**
cooking time **10 minutes**

This recipe from my school days appears regularly in my home as you can make any number of variations in next to no time.

Melt the butter in a frying pan and cook over a moderate heat until it becomes nut brown. Remove from the heat to cool. Place the pan on a damp cloth to stop the cooking.

Sift the flour and sugar with a pinch of salt into a bowl and stir to make a well in the centre.

Beat the egg and milk together and pour into the well. Use a wooden spoon to gradually blend the liquid ingredients into the dry. By incorporating the flour slowly into the egg mixture, you avoid having a lumpy mix. Should lumps arise, beat well and they will break up.

Beat in the cooled browned butter.

Heat a lightly greased frying pan over a moderate heat. Once heated, cook dessertspoonfuls of mixture in the pan for about 1–1½ minutes. Once bubbles appear on the surface and burst, flip the pikelets over and cook for about the same time on the opposite side until they are lightly browned.

Place on a cake rack to cool and cover with a clean tea towel while cooking the remaining mixture.

Serve warm with or without butter or try serving with whipped cream and raspberry jam. Any leftovers can be reheated, under a light cover so they steam, in the microwave for a minute or so to refreshen before serving.

variations

- Add 1–2 tablespoons cocoa to the flour and an extra tablespoon of milk to make a batter of the same consistency.
- Add ½ cup dried fruit and a little flavouring:
  - cranberries or blueberries and orange rind
  - currants and lemon rind
  - sultanas or raisins and mixed spice
- Add about ½ cup finely diced fresh fruits like apple, pear, banana, feijoa, blueberries or raspberries, ripe peaches or nectarines.
- Add ½ cup chocolate chips – try a mix of dark and white chocolate chips and add a few drops of vanilla essence.

L:R:
basic pikelets
ricotta & herb pikelets (page 118)

allyson's tip

Ricotta was originally only made from the whey – the watery part – left over from making cheese. Today, though, it is often enriched with milk or cream. It is a white blandish cheese, often with little grainy bits and a slight sweet note. Ricotta varies greatly depending on the brand purchased and so more liquid may need to be added to make a batter that is thick yet pourable.

1 cup self-raising flour
½ teaspoon salt
200 grams ricotta
1 egg
1 cup milk

2 tablespoons chopped fresh herbs (oregano and basil make a nice combination)
25 grams butter, melted

1 cup flour
½ teaspoon baking powder
1 tablespoon sugar
1 egg, separated
1 cup plain unsweetened yoghurt
¼ cup milk
1 teaspoon vanilla essence
50 grams butter, melted
1 medium-sized apple peeled, cored and finely diced

cinnamon sugar
¼ cup sugar (caster sugar is best)
1 teaspoon ground cinnamon

glazed apples
2 apples, cored and sliced
sugar

ricotta & herb pikelets

makes 16–18
preparation time **10 minutes**
cooking time **10 minutes**

Simply delicious. Try topped with smoked salmon and a small dollop of crème fraîche for an easy nibble to have with drinks.

Sift the flour and salt into a bowl and make a well in the centre.

In a separate jug or bowl, beat together the ricotta, egg, milk and herbs and pour into the well. Gradually blend to a smoothish batter with a wooden spoon. Lastly add the melted butter.

Heat a lightly greased frying pan over a moderate heat. Once heated place tablespoonfuls of mixture into the pan and cook for about 1 minute or until bubbles appear and burst on the surface.

Flip the pikelets and cook for about the same time on the opposite side until they are lightly browned.

Place on a cake rack to cool and cover with a clean tea towel while cooking the remaining mixture.

Serve warm as is or with softened butter spread on top. Add a few chopped fresh herbs or a little grated lemon rind to the butter if wished.

Pictured on previous page.

apple waffles

makes 6
preparation time **15 minutes**
cooking time **15 minutes**

Sift the flour, baking powder and sugar into a bowl and make a well in the centre.

Mix together the egg yolk, yoghurt, milk and vanilla essence and pour into the well. Use a wooden spoon to mix together.

In a clean bowl, beat the egg white until stiff and fold into the batter with the melted butter and diced apple.

Heat a waffle-iron and grease lightly. Cook half-cupfuls of mixture at a time. If you do not have a waffle-iron, make pancakes, cooking the mixture in batches in a moderately hot, lightly greased frying pan. Keep warm in a low oven while cooking all the batter.

Serve the waffles with cinnamon sugar and glazed apples.

cinnamon sugar
Shake or stir the ingredients together.

glazed apples
Cook the apple slices in a knob of butter in a frying pan turning until lightly browned. Sprinkle with a little sugar and turn until the sugar melts and the slices are glazed.

apple waffles

1½ cups self-raising flour
50 grams butter
3 eggs, separated
2 cups buttermilk
1½ cups frozen cranberries, defrosted

yankee buttermilk pancakes

makes 6
preparation time **15 minutes**
cooking time **15 minutes**

This pancake is deliciously light in texture and without sugar it can be enjoyed sweet dusted with icing sugar or savoury with crispy bacon and maple syrup.

Sift the flour into a bowl and make a well in the centre.

Melt the butter in a frying pan and cook until it is nut brown in colour. Remove from the heat and place on a cold wet cloth to stop any further browning. Cool.

Mix the egg yolks with the buttermilk and pour into the well.

Gradually stir together, adding the butter at the end.

In a clean bowl, whisk the egg whites until they form thick soft peaks. Fold into the batter with a slotted spoon.

Cook ¾ cupfuls of the batter in a moderately hot greased pan. Scatter ¼ cup of cranberries over the pancake. (Added this way the berries will stay whole and each pancake will have an equal amount.) When the bubbles on the top of the surface begin to burst, turn the pancake over and cook the other side for a further 1–2 minutes.

Serve warm accompanied with whipped cream and extra defrosted cranberries, if wished, and dusted with icing sugar.

½ cup flour
1 egg
about ¾ cup milk

basic crêpes

makes 6
preparation time **40 minutes** (includes standing time)
cooking time **15 minutes**

Crêpes are traditional thin French pancakes. I enjoy them with freshly squeezed lemon juice and sugar, then rolled up like a cigar and served with whipped cream.

Sift the flour with a pinch of salt into a bowl. Make a well in the centre.

Beat the egg and milk together and strain to remove any lumps of egg.

Pour the liquid into the well, stirring with a wooden spoon to make a smooth batter. The batter should be of pouring consistency. Add extra milk if necessary.

Strain the batter into a jug and allow to stand for about 30 minutes.

Pour sufficient batter into the base of a moderately-hot greased pancake pan so that when the pan is rotated the batter just covers the base with a thin layer.

When the crêpe surface begins to look dull on the top and the bottom is brown, flip the crêpe over and cook the other side only until it is browned (about one minute). Stack the crêpes on top of each other until ready to eat.

Serve sprinkled with caster sugar and freshly squeezed lemon juice.

allyson's tip

To freeze pancakes and crêpes, place a piece of paper between each layer. This will help separate each layer easily when defrosting.

did you know?

Pancakes hold a special place in Easter celebrations. On Shrove Tuesday, the last day before Lent, the cupboards would be cleaned in readiness for fasting. Pancakes were thus made with these ingredients and no doubt greatly enjoyed.

loaves

150 grams butter, softened
½ cup grated palm sugar
¼ cup sugar
grated rind of 3 limes or 2 lemons
2 eggs
2¼ cups self-raising flour, sifted
1 cup mashed ripe bananas
¼ cup milk
¼ cup pecans or walnuts, optional

lime glaze
1 cup icing sugar
2–3 tablespoons freshly squeezed lime
   or lemon juice

palm sugar
& lime banana loaf

makes 1 loaf
preparation time **20 minutes**
cooking time **45–50 minutes**

Palm sugar adds a warm caramel flavour to this tropics-inspired banana loaf.

Preheat the oven to 180 °C. Grease and line the base of a large (21-cm x 11-cm) loaf tin.

Beat the butter, palm sugar, sugar and lime or lemon rind together until soft and creamy.

Beat in the eggs one at a time, beating well after each addition.

Gently fold in the flour, banana and milk.

Turn into the prepared loaf tin and top with pecans or walnuts, if using.

Bake in the preheated oven for 45–50 minutes until a skewer inserted comes out clean.

Turn onto a cake rack and cover with the lime glaze. Decorate with shredded lemon or lime rind, if wished. Serve sliced.

Keep in an airtight container.

lime glaze
Sift the icing sugar and mix in the lime or lemon juice.

Use well-dried packaged dates not the fresh dried dates found in the fruit and vegetable aisle, as these are too moist and the recipe will not be successful.

L–R:
breakfast tea fruit loaf
date loaf

1 cup cold tea
1½ cups mixed dried fruit
grated rind of 1 orange
½ cup honey

2 cups self-raising flour
1 teaspoon baking powder
½ cup rolled oats
50 grams butter, well-softened

1 cup chopped dried dates
1 teaspoon baking soda
1 cup hot tea
2 tablespoons butter
¾ cup sugar

1 egg, beaten
2 cups flour
2 teaspoons baking powder
½ cup chopped walnuts,
    optional

breakfast tea fruit loaf

makes 1 loaf
preparation time **30 minutes**
cooking time **45–55 minutes**

The tea needs to be well brewed to add flavour to this loaf. Try an Irish breakfast or Russian caravan tea – both are strong teas.

Preheat the oven to 170 °C. Grease and line the base of a medium (22-cm x 9-cm) loaf tin.

Pour the cold tea over the dried fruit. Stir in the orange rind and honey and leave to stand for 20 minutes.

In a medium-sized bowl, sift together the flour and baking powder and stir in the oats. Make a well in the centre.

Pour in the fruit mixture, add the butter and mix gently with a wooden spoon until just combined.

Transfer to the prepared loaf tin.

Bake in the preheated oven for 45–55 minutes until well risen and golden and a skewer inserted comes out clean.

Stand in the tin for 10 minutes before turning out onto a cake rack to cool. Wrap in foil and keep for 1–2 days before slicing, so the mellow flavour of the honey can come through.

date loaf

makes 1 loaf
preparation time **60 minutes** (includes cooling time)
cooking time **40 minutes**

In my childhood a date loaf was always a solid stand-by to have in the cupboard and I remember clearly this was one of the first recipes my mum taught me to cook. I enjoy it spread with butter, and if it gets a bit stale, toast it – it's just wonderful.

In a bowl, mix together dates, baking soda and hot tea. Leave to stand for 1 hour or until cool.

Preheat the oven to 180 °C. Grease and line the base of a medium (22-cm x 9-cm) loaf tin.

Using a wooden spoon, mix the butter and sugar together, the mixture will not cream but it needs to be well mixed.

Gradually beat in the egg a little at a time until well mixed in.

Sift the flour and baking powder together. Stir the date mixture into the butter mixture alternately with the flour and nuts, if adding. Turn into the prepared loaf tin.

Bake in the preheated oven for about 40 minutes or until a skewer inserted comes out clean.

Allow to stand in the tin for 10 minutes before turning out onto a cake rack to cool. Store in an airtight container.

allyson's tip

To defrost frozen berries, place them in a single layer on an absorbent paper-lined plate, cover and leave for about 30 minutes or until defrosted. Do not leave to get too warm as the berries will lose too much juice.

L–R:
lemon & pecan loaf
cranberry & orange loaf

175 grams butter, softened
1 cup caster sugar
1 tablespoon finely grated lemon rind
3 eggs
½ cup sour cream
2 cups flour

3 teaspoons baking powder
½ cup fresh lemon juice
½ cup pecans, roughly chopped

lemon syrup
¼ cup caster sugar
½ cup fresh lemon juice

100 grams butter, softened
1 cup sugar (caster is best)
grated rind of 1 orange
2 eggs
2 cups flour
1 teaspoon baking soda

½ teaspoon baking powder
1 cup buttermilk or light sour cream
1 cup frozen cranberries, defrosted
½ cup shredded coconut

lemon & pecan loaf

makes 1 loaf
preparation time **20 minutes**
cooking time **1 hour**

The richness and sweetness of this delightful loaf is tempered by a biting lemon syrup. Try warm as a dessert with whipped cream.

Preheat the oven to 170 °C. Grease and line the bottom of a large (21-cm x 11-cm) loaf tin.

In a large bowl, beat the butter, sugar and lemon rind together until light and fluffy. Add the eggs one at a time, beating well after each addition. Beat in the sour cream.

Sift together the flour and baking powder and fold into the creamed mixture alternately with the lemon juice and most of the pecans. Turn into the prepared loaf tin and scatter the remaining pecans on top.

Bake in the preheated oven for 1 hour or until well risen, golden and a skewer inserted in the centre comes out clean. While the loaf is cooking prepare the syrup.

Spoon the warm lemon syrup slowly over the hot loaf, then allow the loaf to cool and absorb the syrup before turning out to cool thoroughly. Serve thickly sliced.

lemon syrup
Dissolve the sugar in the lemon juice over a low heat, boil rapidly for 2–3 minutes.

cranberry & orange loaf

makes 1 loaf
preparation time **15 minutes**
cooking time **55–60 minutes**

Cranberries add a special touch to this loaf.

Preheat the oven to 170 °C. Grease and line the bottom of a large (21-cm x 11-cm) loaf tin.

In a large bowl, beat together the butter, sugar and orange rind until light and creamy.

Add the eggs one at a time, beating well after each addition.

Sift together the flour, baking soda and baking powder.

Fold into the creamed mixture alternately with the buttermilk or light sour cream. Gently fold in the cranberries towards the end.

Transfer the mixture to the prepared loaf tin and scatter over the coconut.

Bake in the preheated oven for 55–60 minutes until the loaf is golden and a skewer inserted comes out clean. If the coconut begins to over-brown, cover the loaf with a piece of paper.

Leave in the tin to cool for 10 minutes before transferring to a cake rack. Serve thickly sliced. Keep in an airtight container.

Do you know that country where lemon-trees flower,
And oranges of gold glow in the dark leaves,
And a gentle breeze blows from the blue heaven?
– Goethe, *Wilhelm Meister*

¾ cup milk
½ cup poppy seeds
150 grams butter, softened
¾ cup sugar
2 eggs
1¾ cups flour
1 teaspoon baking powder
1 teaspoon baking soda

2 teaspoons grated lemon rind
¼ cup freshly squeezed lemon juice

rich lemon butter icing
75 grams butter, softened
¾ cup icing sugar, sifted
1 teaspoon grated lemon rind
2–3 teaspoons freshly squeezed lemon juice

lemon & poppy seed loaf

makes 1 loaf
preparation time **45 minutes** (includes cooling)
cooking time **1 hour**

Poppy seeds are more often seen atop bread, but they are delicious in sweet baking, especially when married with lemon.

Heat the milk in a small saucepan and when hot but not boiling, stir in the poppy seeds. Set aside to cool for 30 minutes.

Preheat the oven to 180 °C. Grease and line a small (18-cm x 8-cm) loaf tin with baking paper.

In a medium-sized bowl, beat the butter and sugar until light and creamy. Add the eggs one at a time, beating well after each addition.

Sift the flour with the baking powder and baking soda and fold into the creamed mixture alternately with the poppy seeds and milk, lemon rind and juice.

Turn into the prepared loaf tin.

Bake in the preheated oven for 1 hour or until a skewer inserted comes out clean. Allow the loaf to stand for 10 minutes before turning out onto a cake rack to cool.

Ice with the rich lemon butter icing when cold and decorate with extra grated lemon rind, if wished.

rich lemon butter icing

Beat the butter and icing sugar together until smooth and pale in colour. Add the lemon rind and enough juice to make a smooth icing of spreadable consistency.

1½ cups self-raising flour
1 teaspoon ground ginger
50 grams butter, diced
½ cup brown sugar
½ cup chopped dried figs
½ cup milk
¼ cup orange marmalade
1 egg, lightly beaten
2 tablespoons glacé peel, optional

marmalade &
fig tea bread

makes 1 loaf
preparation time **15 minutes**
cooking time **50–55 minutes**

This loaf keeps well and is delicious thickly sliced and topped with butter and more marmalade.

Preheat the oven to 170 °C. Grease and line the base of a large (21-cm x 11-cm) loaf tin.

Sift the flour and ginger into a medium-sized bowl and rub in the butter until the mixture resembles fine breadcrumbs. Stir in the sugar and figs.

In a separate jug or bowl, mix together the milk, marmalade and egg. Stir into the dry ingredients and mix gently with a slotted spoon to form a soft batter.

Turn the mixture into the prepared loaf tin, level the surface with a spatula and scatter over the mixed peel, if using.

Bake in the preheated oven for 50–55 minutes until golden brown and a skewer inserted in the centre comes out clean.

variations
- Vary the dried fruit, trying prunes or raisins.
- In place of ginger, use mixed spice.
- Add a touch of rum or brandy by substituting 2 or 3 tablespoons of milk for your preferred spirit.
- Try apricot jam in place of the marmalade.
- To make this loaf dairy free, use ¼ cup light-flavoured oil in place of the butter and soy or goat's milk in place of milk.

Love and scandal are the best sweetners of tea.
– Henry Fielding

1½ cups self-raising flour
1 cup sugar
½ teaspoon baking powder
¾ cup desiccated coconut
1 cup thick natural unsweetened yoghurt
2 eggs, beaten

2 tablespoons dark rum
75 grams butter, melted

passion-fruit icing
25 grams butter, melted
pulp of 2 ripe passion-fruit,
1¼–1½ cups icing sugar, sifted

yoghurt & coconut loaf

makes 1 loaf
preparation time 20 minutes
cooking time 1 hour

This loaf is perfect for a morning-tea treat.

Preheat the oven to 180 °C. Grease and line the base and sides of a small (18-cm x 8-cm) loaf tin.

In a large bowl, sift together the flour, sugar and baking powder. Stir in the coconut and make a well in the centre.

In a separate jug or bowl, beat together the yoghurt, eggs and rum and pour into the well of the dry ingredients.

Stir together gently, adding the butter.

Turn the mixture into the prepared loaf tin.

Bake in the preheated oven for 1 hour or until a skewer inserted comes out clean.

Stand the cake for 10 minutes before turning out onto a cake rack to cool.

When cold, spread the top with passion-fruit icing and serve in thick slices.

passion-fruit icing
Mix the melted butter with the passion-fruit pulp. Gradually beat in sufficient icing sugar to make a soft, slightly runny icing.

2 cups self-raising flour
1 teaspoon mixed spice
1 cup mashed peeled feijoas
¾ cup honey
1 egg
grated rind of 1 orange
100 grams butter, softened

feijoa & honey loaf

makes 1 loaf
preparation time **15 minutes**
cooking time **45 minutes**

Set the oven rack in the centre of the oven. Preheat the oven to 180 °C. Grease and line the base of a medium (22-cm x 9-cm) loaf tin with baking paper.

In a medium-sized bowl, sift together the flour and mixed spice. Make a well in the centre by pushing the flour out to the edges of the bowl.

In a jug, beat together the mashed feijoas, honey, egg and orange rind and pour into the well.

Add the butter and beat well for one minute with a wooden spoon until soft and whipped in texture.

Transfer to the prepared loaf tin and level off.

Bake in the preheated oven for 45 minutes or until a skewer inserted comes out clean.

Remove from the oven and stand for 10 minutes before turning out onto a cake rack to cool.

Serve warm, thickly sliced or cold and lightly buttered.

The King was in his counting house
counting out his money,
The Queen was in the parlour
eating bread and honey.

175 grams butter, softened
¾ cup caster sugar
2 teaspoons vanilla essence
3 eggs, lightly beaten
½ cup flour
¾ cup self-raising flour
1–2 tablespoons milk
glacé peel to decorate, optional

madeira loaf

makes 1 loaf
preparation time **15 minutes**
cooking time **35–40 minutes**

A simple plain loaf that keeps well and remains moist.

Preheat the oven to 180 °C. Grease and line the base of a medium (22-cm x 9-cm) loaf tin with baking paper.

In a medium-sized bowl, beat the butter, sugar and vanilla essence until light and creamy.

Gradually beat in the eggs a little at a time.

Sift the flours together and gently fold into the creamed mixture with a slotted metal spoon. Add a little milk if necessary to give a cake batter of dropping consistency.

Turn into the prepared cake tin and level off. Decorate with glacé peel, if using.

Bake in the preheated oven for 35–40 minutes until well risen, golden and a skewer inserted in the middle comes out clean.

Allow the loaf to stand in the tin for 10 minutes before turning out onto a cake rack to cool completely. Keep in an airtight container.

variations
ʓ• Decorate the top of the loaf with citrus peel, glacé fruit or walnuts before baking.
ʓ• Add the grated rind of 1 large orange.
ʓ• Dust with icing sugar before slicing and serving.

muffins, cup cakes & small cakes

3 cups flour
¾ cup sugar
1 teaspoon baking powder
1 teaspoon baking soda
2 oranges
1½ cups plain unsweetened yoghurt
2 eggs
2 cups finely sliced rhubarb
100 grams butter, melted

rhubarb & orange muffins

makes 12–16 standard muffins
preparation time **20 minutes**
cooking time **20–25 minutes**

Rhubarb is one fruit that can easily be grown in your garden or in a large tub and harvested almost all year round – making great tarts, crumbles, cakes and muffins.

Place the oven rack in the centre of the oven. Preheat the oven to 200 °C. Grease 12–16 standard muffin cups or line with paper cases.

In a large bowl, sift together the flour, sugar, baking powder and baking soda and make a well in the centre.

Grate the rind from the oranges and set aside. Cut away all the bitter white pith and discard. Roughly chop the flesh.

In a food processor, blend together the orange rind and flesh, yoghurt and eggs until smooth.

Pour into the well and stir gently into the dry ingredients with the rhubarb and butter.

Divide the mixture evenly among the prepared muffin cups.

Bake in the preheated oven for 20–25 minutes or until golden and firm to the touch.

Serve warm with butter or whipped cream.

allyson's tips

- If you are using older thicker stalks of rhubarb, remove any coarse outer strings before slicing.
- Spices that marry well with rhubarb include ginger, vanilla and cinnamon. Add a little of these to the muffin recipe.

did you know?

- Rhubarb is actually a vegetable. In the late 1940s the US Customs Department formally classified it as a fruit.

2 cups flour
4 teaspoons baking powder
¾ cup sugar (caster is best)
1¼ cups milk
2 eggs
½ cup finely chopped, peeled fresh
    feijoas
100 grams butter, melted and cooled

lime glaze
2 tablespoons sugar
2 tablespoons orange juice or water
grated rind and juice of 2 limes

feijoa muffins
with lime glaze

makes 12 standard muffins
preparation time 15 minutes
cooking time 15–20 minutes

Feijoas make wonderful partners to tart limes in rich muffin batter.

Preheat the oven to 190 °C. Grease 12 standard muffin cups or line with paper cases.

In a large bowl, sift together the flour, baking powder and sugar and make a well in the centre.

In a jug, beat together the milk, eggs and feijoas. Pour into the dry ingredients.

Using a slotted spoon, fold together with the butter.

Divide the mixture evenly among the prepared muffin cups.

Bake in the preheated oven for 15–20 minutes until golden brown and the centre of the muffin springs back when touched.

Stand for 1 minute before brushing each muffin with a little of the lime glaze. Stand for a further 2–3 minutes before serving warm.

lime glaze
Simmer the sugar, orange juice or water and lime rind and juice together until the sugar has dissolved.

Do you know the muffin man,
The muffin man, the muffin man?
Do you know the muffin man,
Who lives in Drury lane?

tamarillo & cinnamon muffins

❧ To blanch a tamarillo, make a shallow cross in the base of the tamarillo. Plunge into boiling water for about 1 minute – the skin will split. Plunge into cold water and when cool enough to handle, peel the skin away.

❧ When buying tamarillos, make sure the stalks are green and not dark and dry, that the calyx is attached and there is no green skin around the calyx as this means the fruit will not ripen and the flavour will be inferior.

orange & date muffins

❧ If preparing without a food processor, grate the rind from the orange, discard the bitter pith and chop the flesh finely. Mix all ingredients together gently in a bowl.

Rear: tamarillo & cinnamon muffins
Front: orange & date muffins

5 tamarillos, blanched and peeled
3 cups flour
¾ cup sugar
2 teaspoons baking powder
1 teaspoon baking soda
1 tablespoon ground cinnamon
1 cup sour cream or yoghurt
2 eggs
¾ cup milk
100 grams butter, melted

cinnamon sugar topping
2 tablespoons butter, melted
1 tablespoon sugar (caster is best)
1 teaspoon ground cinnamon

tamarillo & cinnamon muffins

makes 18 standard muffins
preparation time 20 minutes
cooking time 18–20 minutes

Preheat the oven to 200 °C. Lightly grease 18 standard muffin cups or line with paper cases.

Dice 4 tamarillos finely. Cut the remaining tamarillo into 6 wedge-style slices, then slice each crosswise in thirds. Set aside for topping.

In a large bowl, sift the flour, sugar, baking powder, baking soda and cinnamon and make a well in the centre.

In a jug, beat together the sour cream or yoghurt, eggs and milk.

Pour into the well of the dry ingredients with the butter and diced tamarillos and stir together gently with a slotted spoon.

Divide evenly among the prepared muffin cups and place a piece of tamarillo on top.

Bake in the preheated oven for 18–20 minutes until well risen and golden.

Remove from the oven and brush the hot muffins with the melted butter. Mix the sugar and cinnamon together and sprinkle evenly on top.

1 large orange
1 egg
½ cup sugar (caster is best)
½ cup well-packed dates
125 grams butter, melted and cooled
½ cup yoghurt (plain or fruit)
½ cup milk
2 cups flour
1 teaspoon baking soda
1 teaspoon baking powder

orange & date muffins

makes 12 standard muffins
preparation time 15 minutes
cooking time 15–18 minutes

This recipe is from my time as a junior home economist at the _New Zealand Woman's Weekly_ in the early 1980s.

Preheat the oven to 190 °C. Grease 12 standard muffin cups or line with paper cases.

Grate the rind from the orange. With a small knife peel away the bitter white orange pith that remains and discard. Chop the orange flesh roughly.

Put the orange flesh, rind, egg and sugar into a food processor and process for 1–2 minutes until well blended. Add the dates, butter, yoghurt and milk. Pulse until the dates are well chopped.

Sift flour, baking soda and baking powder and sprinkle evenly over the top of the liquid ingredients in the food processor. Pulse only until all ingredients are mixed.

Spoon the mixture into the prepared muffin cups.

Bake in the preheated oven for 15–18 minutes until the orange and date muffins are golden brown and well cooked. Cool in the tin for 2–3 minutes before serving.

variations
❧ Use raisins or sultanas in place of dates.

250 grams butter, softened
1 cup brown sugar
½ cup honey
3 eggs
2½ cups flour
4 teaspoons baking soda

2 teaspoons mixed spice
2½ cups wheat bran
1 cup plain unsweetened yoghurt
1½ cups milk
250 grams dried dates or raisins,
  finely chopped

sarah's bran muffins

makes 18 standard muffins
preparation time 20 minutes
cooking time 25 minutes

These bran muffins are light and tender. Ideal for a treat with a smidgen of health added in – well, maybe! This recipe is adapted from a much-loved book from the '80s – *Open House* by Sarah Leah Chase.

Preheat the oven to 190 °C. Grease 18 standard muffin cups or line with paper cases.

In a large bowl, beat the butter, sugar and honey together until very light and creamy.

Add the eggs one at a time, beating well after each addition.

Sift flour, baking soda and spice together and fold into the creamed mixture with the bran, yoghurt, milk and dried fruit.

Divide the mixture evenly among the prepared cups.

Bake in the preheated oven for 25 minutes or until well risen and firm to the touch.

Serve hot and lightly buttered.

variations
- Try ground ginger and diced glacé pears.
- Use a mix of bran and wheat germ.
- Use golden or maple syrup in place of honey.

allyson's tip
Keep bran in the refrigerator as it will become rancid quickly in a hot pantry.

family chocolate chip muffins

2 cups self-raising flour
125 grams butter, diced
½ cup sugar
1 cup chocolate chips
½ cup milk
½ cup sour cream
2 eggs
2 tablespoons golden syrup

2½ cups flour
¼ cup sugar
1½ teaspoons baking powder
1 teaspoon baking soda
1 cup milk
½ sour cream
125 grams butter, melted and
    cooled
1 egg
2 cups blueberries, fresh or
    frozen and defrosted

family chocolate chip muffins

makes 16 standard muffins
preparation time 10 minutes
cooking time 15–18 minutes

Preheat the oven to 190 °C. Grease 16 standard muffin cups or line with paper cases.

Sift flour in a bowl. Rub in the butter until the mixture resembles fine crumbs.

Stir in the sugar and chocolate chips and make a well in the centre.

In a jug or bowl, beat together the milk, sour cream, eggs and golden syrup.

Pour into the well and mix together gently with a slotted spoon. Do not over-mix.

Divide the mixture evenly among the prepared muffin cups.

Bake in the preheated oven for 15–18 minutes until well risen and golden. Stand in the tin for 2–3 minutes before serving.

blueberry muffins

makes 12 standard muffins
preparation time 15 minutes
cooking time 12–15 minutes

Rich in anti-oxidants, the blueberry is something of a super-food and is delicious in these tasty muffins.

Preheat the oven to 190 °C. Grease 12 standard muffin cups or line with paper cases.

In a large bowl, sift together the flour, sugar, baking powder and baking soda and make a well in the centre.

In a separate jug, mix together the milk, sour cream, butter and egg until smooth.

Pour the liquid ingredients into the well and add the blueberries.

Using a slotted spoon, mix gently and only until all ingredients are incorporated. Do not over-mix as the muffins will peak.

Spoon the muffin mixture evenly among the prepared muffin cups.

Bake in the preheated oven for 12–15 minutes or until the muffins are golden and cooked. Serve warm with butter or whipped sweetened cream cheese on the side.

Pictured overleaf.

allyson's tips

sugar 'n' spice apple muffins
- Sprinkle the apple pie spice on top of these muffins for a delicious change. (See page 18.)

- Use diced canned apple – it makes these muffins in no time. Alternatively, use 1 cup finely diced raw apple.

banana & honey muffins
- 2 medium-sized bananas, mashed, is about ¾ cup.

- Use a mild-flavoured honey here; strong-flavoured honeys will be too over-powering for the other delicate ingredients.

L–R:
blueberry muffins (page 153)
banana & honey muffins
sugar 'n' spice apple muffins

3 cups flour
2 tablespoons baking powder
¾ cup sugar (caster is nice)
1 teaspoon each ground ginger
and mixed spice
1½ cups milk
1½ cups diced cooked apple
2 eggs
few drops vanilla essence
½ cup sultanas, optional

100 grams butter, melted and
cooled
16–18 walnut halves, optional

sugar 'n' spice topping
juice of 1 lemon or 2
tablespoons butter, melted
1 tablespoon sugar
(caster is best)
1 teaspoon mixed spice

100 grams butter, softened
½ cup brown sugar
½ cup runny honey
2 eggs
grated rind of 1 lemon
1½ cups flour

2 teaspoons baking soda
1 teaspoon baking powder
1 cup wheat germ
½ cup non-fat plain yoghurt
1 cup milk
¾ cup mashed bananas

sugar 'n' spice apple muffins

makes 16–18 standard muffins
preparation time **15 minutes**
cooking time **20 minutes**

We cook these for friends regularly and they are always a huge success. For something different, serve them hot with cream or custard as a dessert, almost like a mini steamed pudding!

Preheat the oven to 200 °C. Grease 16–18 standard muffin cups or line with paper cases.

Sift the flour, baking powder, sugar and spices into a bowl and make a well in the centre.

Beat together the milk, apple, eggs and vanilla essence. Fold into the dry ingredients, adding the sultanas, if using, and butter towards the end of mixing.

Three-quarters fill the prepared muffin cups and decorate each muffin with a walnut half, if using.

Bake in the preheated oven for 20 minutes or until well risen, golden and cooked.

Remove muffins from the oven and brush with the lemon juice or melted butter. Mix the sugar and mixed spice together and sprinkle over the top. Serve warm.

variation
❧• Use pears in place of apples.

banana & honey muffins

makes 12–16 standard muffins
preparation time **15 minutes**
cooking time **15–18 minutes**

Studded with wheat germ and sweetened with honey, these banana muffins are incredibly light with plenty of yum factor.

Preheat the oven to 200 °C. Lightly grease 12–16 standard muffin cups or line with paper cases.

Beat together the butter, sugar, honey, eggs and lemon rind until well combined. This can also be done in a food processor.

Sift the flour, baking soda and baking powder into a large bowl and stir through the wheat germ and make a well in the centre.

Pour the butter mixture into the well with the yoghurt, milk and bananas and stir all the ingredients together gently with a slotted spoon.

Three-quarters fill the prepared muffin cups.

Bake in the preheated oven for 15–18 minutes or until well risen. Stand for one minute in the tins before transferring to a cake rack to cool. Serve warm drizzled with honey or with cream cheese sweetened with honey.

variation
❧• Make the recipe with bran in place of wheat germ.

125 grams dark chocolate, chopped
¼ cup cream
1¾ cups flour
½ cup caster sugar
¼ cup cocoa
1½ teaspoons baking powder

½ teaspoon baking soda
½ cup non-fat plain yoghurt
½ cup milk
1 egg
75 grams butter, melted

double chocolate muffins

makes 12 muffins or 6 mini cakes
preparation time **30 minutes**
cooking time **15–18 minutes**

allyson's tip

For cup cakes, three-quarters fill 6 mini cake paper cases. Bake at 190 °C for 20–25 minutes. Serve warm with chocolate cream topping (see page 30) and decorate as wished.

Rich chocolate muffins with a rich chocolate fudge centre. An absolute treat for chocoholics!

Preheat the oven to 200 °C. Grease 12 standard muffin cups or line with paper cases.

Place the chocolate and cream in a microwave-proof jug and microwave for 1 minute on high (100%) or until the chocolate has almost melted. Stir well and leave until cool enough to roll into 12 even-shaped balls, each about the size of a cherry.

In a large bowl, sift the flour, sugar, cocoa, baking powder and baking soda and make a well in the centre.

In a jug, beat together the yoghurt, milk and egg. Pour into the well and stir into the dry ingredients, folding in the butter at the end.

Half fill the prepared muffin cups with the mixture. Place a chocolate fudge ball in each and top each with an equal amount of the remaining muffin mix.

Bake in the preheated oven for 15–18 minutes until well risen and cooked.

Cool in the tin for 5 minutes before dusting with icing sugar to serve.

2 cups flour
2 teaspoons baking powder
1 teaspoon baking soda
½ teaspoon white pepper
1 ham steak, finely diced
½ cup pine nuts, toasted, optional

1 cup plain unsweetened yoghurt
1 cup milk
¼ cup oil or melted butter
2 eggs
¼ cup basil pesto
50 grams Brie or Camembert

2 cups self-raising flour
½ teaspoon each salt and pepper
½ teaspoon baking powder
1¼ cups grated Cheddar-style cheese
½ cup milk
½ cup plain unsweetened yoghurt
¼ cup tomato paste (sun-dried or plain)

1 egg
¼ cup oil or melted butter
2 tablespoons diced black olives
2 tablespoons finely diced sun-dried tomatoes
2 tablespoons finely chopped fresh parsley or celery leaves
¼ cup finely sliced salami

pesto & ham muffins

makes **12 standard muffins**
preparation time **15 minutes**
cooking time **18–20 minutes**

These muffins are perfect with a chilled glass of white wine on any summer's afternoon, or with a coffee and grilled bacon and tomato for brunch.

Place the oven rack in the centre of the oven. Preheat the oven to 220 °C. Grease 12 standard muffin cups or line with paper cases.

In a large bowl, sift the flour, baking powder, baking soda and white pepper. Stir through the diced ham and pine nuts (if using). Make a well in the centre.

In a jug, beat together the yoghurt, milk, oil or melted butter, eggs and pesto. Pour into the well and stir together gently with a slotted spoon.

Divide the mixture evenly among the prepared muffin cups. Cut the cheese into 12 thin slices and place a piece on top of each muffin.

Bake in the preheated oven for 18–20 minutes until well risen, golden and cooked. Cool in the tin for 2–3 minutes before serving.

variations
- Use sun-dried tomato pesto in place of basil pesto.
- Use just under 1 cup of finely diced smoked chicken in place of the ham.

pizza muffins

makes **12 standard muffins**
preparation time **15 minutes**
cooking time **18–20 minutes**

All the flavours of your favourite pizza encased in a tender muffin. Serve warm with a glass of wine.

Preheat the oven to 200 °C. Grease 12 standard muffin cups or line with paper cases.

In a large bowl, sift together the flour, salt, pepper and baking powder. Stir in one cup of the cheese.

In a separate bowl, mix together the milk, yoghurt, tomato paste, egg, oil or melted butter, olives, sun-dried tomatoes and parsley or celery leaves.

Pour into the dry ingredients and, using a slotted spoon, mix together gently with the salami.

Divide evenly among the prepared mufffin cups and top each muffin with a little of the remaining grated cheese.

Bake in the preheated oven for 18–20 minutes until golden and cooked. Cool 1–2 minutes before serving.

L–R:
pesto & ham muffins
pizza muffins

2 cups flour
4 teaspoons baking powder
1 teaspoon paprika
½ teaspoon salt
½ teaspoon ground black pepper
50 grams butter
1 cup tasty Cheddar-style cheese, grated

2 tablespoons each of fresh thyme and fresh oregano, chopped (or 1 teaspoon each dried)
1¼ cups milk
1 egg
250 grams Camembert

hot camembert stuffed mini muffins

makes **24 mini muffins**
preparation time **20 minutes**
cooking time **10–12 minutes**

These jazzed-up mini cheese muffins are a delightful savoury nibble.

Preheat the oven to 200 °C. Line 24 mini muffin cups with paper cases.

In a large bowl, sift the flour, baking powder, paprika, salt and pepper.

Rub in the butter until it resembles crumbs. Stir in the grated cheese and herbs and make a well in the centre.

In a separate jug, beat the milk and egg together and pour into the well of the dry ingredients. Stir together gently using a slotted spoon.

Divide mixture evenly among the prepared mini muffin cups.

Bake in the preheated oven for 10–12 minutes until golden brown and cooked. Cool on a cake rack.

Just before serving, cut the Camembert into 24 thin slices. Make a cut in each muffin and fill with a slice of the Camembert.

Bake in a 200 °C oven for 5 minutes until the cheese has just softened.

allyson's tip

Muffins can easily be frozen and reheated for later use. Freeze them in a single layer while fresh in a well-sealed plastic bag and take them out as required. Defrost in the microwave on high power or defrost and reheat in a moderate oven.

125 grams butter, softened *125g*
½ cup caster sugar
1 teaspoon vanilla essence
2 eggs, beaten
1¼ cups self-raising flour, sifted

¼ cup milk
1 quantity butter icing
  (see page 29)
12 glacé cherries

315g

basic cup cakes

makes 12 cup cakes
preparation time 15 minutes
cooking time 10–12 minutes

From this simple basic recipe you can try any number of variations.

Preheat the oven to 200 °C. Line 12 standard muffin cups with paper cases.

In a bowl beat the butter, sugar and vanilla essence together until light and fluffy. Add the beaten eggs a little at a time, beating well after each addition.

Fold in the sifted flour alternately with the milk. Divide the mixture evenly among the paper cases.

Bake in the preheated oven for 10–12 minutes until well risen and golden. Cool and serve iced with butter icing and garnished with a glacé cherry.

variations

- Rainbow cup cakes – Divide the mixture in thirds. Colour one third pink, another green and the last one blue or yellow. Spoon small amounts of each colour into each paper case – ideal for birthday parties.
- Coconut cup cakes – Replace ¼ cup self-raising flour with desiccated coconut. Ice and decorate with toasted, flaked or thread coconut.
- Coffee cup cakes – Warm the milk and stir in 1 tablespoon of instant coffee granules. Allow to cool before using. Flavour the butter icing with 1–2 teaspoons of coffee granules dissolved in a tablespoon of hot water. Or try a lemon icing – delicious with coffee cakes.
- Cherry cup cakes – Add ½ cup chopped glacé cherries. Colour the icing pink.

125 grams butter, softened
½ cup sugar (caster is best)
1 teaspoon vanilla essence
3 eggs
1 cup all-purpose gluten-free flour
2 teaspoons gluten-free baking powder
¼ cup milk

gluten-free cup cakes

makes 18 cup cakes
preparation time 15 minutes
cooking time 15 minutes

Preheat the oven to 180 °C. Grease 18 standard muffin cups or line with paper cases.

Beat the butter and sugar together until light and creamy.

Add the vanilla essence and the eggs one at a time, beating well after each addition.

In a separate bowl, sift together the gluten-free flour and baking powder. Stir the dry ingredients into the creamed mixture alternately with the milk.

Divide the mixture evenly among the prepared muffin cups.

Bake in the preheated oven for 15 minutes or until well risen and golden.

Cool on a wire rack and decorate with your favourite icing (see pages 28–30).

175 grams butter, softened
½ cup sugar (caster is best)
3 eggs
½ cup lemon curd (home-made is best)
2 cups self-raising flour, sifted
¼ cup milk

lemon curd butterfly cup cakes

makes 12 cup cakes
preparation time 15 minutes
cooking time 20–25 minutes

Place the oven rack in the centre of the oven. Preheat the oven to 190 °C. Line 12 standard muffin cups with paper cases.

Beat the butter and sugar together until light and creamy. Add the eggs one at a time, beating well after each addition. Stir in the lemon curd.

Fold in the flour alternately with the milk.

Divide the mixture evenly among the paper cases.

Bake in the preheated oven for 20–25 minutes until well risen and golden.

Transfer to a cake rack to cool.

Cut a small disc from the centre of each cup cake and cut the disc in half. Fill the cavity with sweetened whipped cream and place two halved discs on top to resemble butterfly wings. Decorate with tiny dollops of lemon curd.

75 grams butter, diced
50 grams dark chocolate, chopped
1 teaspoon instant coffee
2 tablespoons hot water
½ cup brown sugar
2 eggs
1 teaspoon vanilla essence

1 cup self-raising flour
¼ cup cocoa

chocolate cream topping
½ cup cream
150 grams dark chocolate, chopped

chocolate cup cakes

makes 12 cup cakes or 6 mini cakes
preparation time 20 minutes
cooking time 12–15 minutes

Preheat the oven to 180 °C. Line 12 standard muffin cups with paper cases or stand 6 large mini-cake cases on a tray.

In a medium-sized saucepan, stir the butter, chocolate, coffee, hot water and sugar over a low heat until the chocolate has melted and the mixture is smooth. Remove from heat and cool to luke warm.

Beat the eggs together with the vanilla until just mixed and stir into the cooled chocolate mixture.

Sift the flour and cocoa together into a medium-sized bowl and make a well in the centre.

Pour the chocolate mixture into the well of the dry ingredients and stir gently to combine. Do not over-mix.

Divide the mixture evenly among the paper cases.

Bake in the preheated oven for 12–15 minutes until well risen. If baking 6 mini cakes, bake for 20 minutes.

Allow to cool before spreading with chocolate cream topping and decorating as wished.

chocolate cream topping
Heat the cream and chocolate together in a microwave until the cream is warm – about 1 minute on high (100%). Stir until the chocolate has melted. Allow to cool.

The most indispensable ingredient of all good home cooking; love for those you are cooking for.
– Sophia Loren

1½ cups icing sugar
½ cup flour
150 grams ground almonds (about 1 cup)
1 fresh mango
6 egg whites, lightly beaten

175 grams butter, melted and cooled
2 teaspoons vanilla essence
1 teaspoon grated lime rind
1 tablespoon lime juice

mango, almond & lime friands

makes 10 friands
preparation time 15 minutes
cooking time 20–25 minutes

Place the oven rack in the centre of the oven. Preheat the oven to 190 °C. Lightly grease 10 friand or standard muffin cups or line with paper cases.

In a large bowl, sift together the icing sugar and flour. Stir in the ground almonds and make a well in the centre.

Cut the sides from the mango and peel away the skin. Slice one half and dice the other. Set aside.

In a clean bowl, beat the egg whites lightly until they begin to foam. Pour into the dry ingredients with the butter, vanilla essence, lime rind, juice and diced mango and stir together gently.

Three-quarters fill the prepared cups and garnish each with a slice of mango.

Bake in the preheated oven for 20–25 minutes until the friands are firm to the touch and have shrunk from the sides of the tin.

Cool in the tin for 2–3 minutes before turning out onto a cake rack to cool.

Serve warm, dusted with icing sugar and accompanied with mascarpone or sweetened whipped cream.

1¼ cups icing sugar
½ cup flour
150 grams ground almonds (about 1 cup)
100 grams white chocolate, chopped
grated rind of 2 lemons
6 egg whites
175 grams butter, melted and cooled

1 firm ripe pear, peeled and cored

lemon syrup
¼ cup boiling water
¼ cup caster sugar
grated rind of 1 lemon
2 tablespoons lemon juice
2 tablespoons limoncello or lemon vodka, optional

pear & white chocolate friands

makes 10 friands
preparation time 15 minutes
cooking time 20–25 minutes

Place the oven rack in the centre of the oven. Preheat the oven to 180 °C. Lightly grease 10 friand or standard muffin cups or line with paper cases.

Sift the icing sugar and flour into a bowl. Stir in the ground almonds, white chocolate and lemon rind.

In a clean bowl, beat the egg whites lightly until they are frothy. Stir the egg whites and the melted butter into the almond mixture until smooth.

Divide the mixture evenly among the prepared cups. Finely slice the pear and arrange 2–3 pear slices on top of each friand.

Bake in the preheated oven for 20–25 minutes until the friands are firm to the touch and have shrunk a little from the sides of the tin.

Brush the hot friands evenly with the lemon syrup. Leave to cool in the tin before running a knife around the edge and turning the friands onto a cake rack to cool. Dust with icing sugar to serve.

lemon syrup
Stir the boiling water and sugar together until dissolved. If necessary warm in a microwave. Stir in the lemon rind, juice and limoncello or lemon vodka, if using.

Front: mango, almond & lime friands
Behind: pear & white chocolate friands

allyson's tip

- In place of a fresh mango use well-drained canned mangoes or try sliced fresh or canned peaches, apricots or nectarines.

did you know?

- Friand takes its name from the word 'fancier' derived either from the oblong shape of a bar of gold (originally friands were made in bar-shaped tins) or because the cake was popular in Paris's financial district. In New Zealand and Australia we typically bake friands in oval moulds.

100 grams butter, softened
½ cup caster sugar
1 teaspoon vanilla essence
grated rind of 1 lemon or orange
2 eggs
1 cup flour
½ teaspoon baking powder

madeleines

makes 12 madeleines
preparation time **15 minutes**
cooking time **15–18 minutes**

These small French cakes cooked in shallow shell-shaped moulds are at their best when freshly baked. Try them dipped in your favourite fruit tea.

Preheat the oven to 200 °C. Grease and flour 12 madeleine moulds.

In a medium-sized bowl, beat the butter, sugar, vanilla essence and lemon or orange rind until light and fluffy.

Beat in the eggs and continue to beat until mixture is smooth and light.

Sift the flour and baking powder together and carefully stir into the creamed mixture with a slotted spoon.

Divide the mixture evenly among the prepared madeleine moulds.

Bake in the preheated oven for 15–18 minutes until golden and firm to the touch.

Allow the madeleines to cool for 10 minutes before removing from the moulds. Place on a wire rack to cool. Serve dusted with icing sugar and accompanied with mascarpone or sweetened whipped cream.

Eating madeleines, according to the French, will take you back to your childhood.

Sugar and spice and all things nice
– that's what little girls are made of.

1 cup self-raising flour
¼ cup cornflour
1 tablespoon ground ginger
1 teaspoon cinnamon
125 grams butter, softened
½ cup sugar
2 eggs, beaten
1 tablespoon golden syrup

mock cream
50 grams butter, softened
½ cup icing sugar
5–6 tablespoons boiling water

ginger kisses

makes 20 ginger kisses
preparation time 15 minutes
cooking time 10–12 minutes

Ginger kisses are a part of our Kiwi baking heritage. To be really original, fill these with mock cream rather than whipped cream, though to go upmarket you could try mascarpone.

Preheat the oven to 190 °C. Lightly grease 1–2 baking trays or line with baking paper.

Sift the flour, cornflour, ginger and cinnamon together and set aside.

Beat the butter and sugar together until very light. Add the beaten eggs a little at a time and beat well. Beat in the golden syrup.

Fold in the dry ingredients.

Drop dessertspoonfuls of mixture onto the prepared tray. For smaller kisses use heaped teaspoons.

Bake in the preheated oven for 10–12 minutes until the kisses are firm to the touch. Transfer to a cake rack to cool. When cold join with the mock cream.

mock cream
In a small bowl, beat the butter and sugar until light. Gradually beat in the hot water. If the mixture curdles, just keep on beating. Flavour with a touch of vanilla essence, if wished.

150 grams butter, softened
½ cup plus 2 tablespoons sugar
1 teaspoon vanilla essence
2 eggs, beaten
2 cups self-raising flour, sifted
2–3 tablespoons milk
2 cups desiccated or thread
    coconut

thin chocolate icing
2 cups icing sugar
½ cup cocoa
¾ cup hot water
25 grams butter, softened
1–2 teaspoons vanilla essence

snowballs

makes 16 snowballs
preparation time **15 minutes**
cooking time **15 minutes**

A memory from my school days, when we would buy a goodie at the local bakery on the way home from school. The walk was an hour each way – the bakery did a good business!

Place the oven rack in the middle of the oven. Preheat the oven to 190 °C. Lightly grease 16 patty-pans or line with paper cases.

In a medium-sized bowl, beat the butter, sugar and vanilla essence together until well blended.

Add the beaten eggs a little at a time, beating well after each addition. Carefully fold in the flour alternately with the milk.

Spoon the mixture evenly into the prepared patty-pans.

Bake in the preheated oven for 15 minutes or until the cakes are golden and firm to the touch. Transfer to a cake rack to cool.

Place the cake rack over a shallow-sided baking tray. Dip each cake into the thin chocolate icing, allowing any excess to drip off and then toss in the coconut to coat. Return to the cake rack.

Make a slit in the centre of each cake, near the top and fill with sweetened whipped cream. Keep refrigerated in an airtight container once filled with whipped cream.

thin chocolate icing
Sift the icing sugar and cocoa into a bowl. Stir the hot water, butter and vanilla essence together and pour into the dry ingredients. Stir to make a smooth, very thin icing.

½ cup flour
50 grams butter
½ cup water
2 eggs, beaten

cream filling
300 ml cream
2 tablespoons icing sugar
pulp of 1–2 passion-fruit,
    optional

cream puffs

makes 10–12 cream puffs
preparation time **15 minutes**
cooking time **30–35 minutes**

I enjoy these made large and filled with sweetened whipped cream, maybe even flavoured with passion-fruit pulp and covered with chocolate icing . Alternatively, mash up a few strawberries and fold into the cream with a little liqueur.

Place two oven racks either side of the centre. Preheat the oven to 220 °C (fan bake at 200 °C). Grease two oven trays or line with baking paper.

Sift the flour with a pinch of salt onto a plate and have close to the stove.

Cut the butter into small pieces and place into a saucepan with the water. Bring to the boil, ensuring that the butter melts before the mixture boils. If the mixture boils before the butter has melted, there will be too much evaporation, resulting in insufficient liquid when you add the flour.

Tip in all the sifted flour at once and draw off the heat. Beat quickly with a wooden spoon. The mixture should come away from the sides of the saucepan and form a ball.

Allow to cool for about 5 minutes.

Add half the beaten eggs and beat well with a wooden spoon until the mixture is well incorporated. Add the remaining beaten eggs and continue to beat until the mixture is thick and glossy.

Alternatively, put the dough into a food processor and blend in the eggs. Either way will give an excellent result.

Using a soup spoon, drop 10–12 large spoonfuls of mixture onto the prepared trays.

Bake in the preheated oven for 20 minutes. Lower the temperature to 140 °C (120 °C fan bake) for a further 10–15 minutes until the puffs are dry.

Take the puffs from the oven and pierce underneath with the end of a spoon to allow the steam to escape, otherwise they will soften and collapse. For large puffs, return to the oven for 10 minutes once pierced to help dry out the centre. Allow to cool.

Whip the cream and icing sugar together until thick. Add the passion-fruit, if using.

Either cut each puff in half and fill or place the whipped cream into a piping bag and pierce the nozzle through the base of the puff and pipe in the whipped cream.

Top with simple chocolate icing (page 28), if wished, or melted white or dark chocolate.

allyson's tip

For éclairs, fill a piping bag fitted with a star or plain nozzle with the batter-style, choux pastry. Pipe index finger lengths onto the prepared trays. Bake in the preheated oven for 15 minutes before lowering the temperature for 10–15 minutes. Fill and decorate as above.

cakes

175 grams butter, softened
¾ cup caster sugar
1 teaspoon vanilla essence
grated rind of 1 lemon
3 eggs (2 separated, 1 whole)
1½ cups flour, sifted
2 teaspoons baking powder
¼ cup milk
½ cup caster sugar
1 cup desiccated coconut

coconut meringue cake

makes 1 x 20-cm cake
preparation time **15 minutes**
cooking time **40–45 minutes**

All sorts of wonderful things have come out of Australia, including this unusual and delicious cake with a coconut meringue topping.

Set the oven rack just below the centre of the oven. Preheat the oven to 180 °C. Lightly grease, flour and line a 20-cm round or square cake tin.

Beat the butter, first measure of sugar, vanilla essence and lemon rind together in a large bowl until light and creamy.

Beat 2 egg yolks and 1 whole egg into the creamed mixture.

Fold the sifted flour and baking powder into the creamed mixture alternately with the milk.

Turn the mixture into the prepared cake tin.

In a clean bowl, beat the 2 egg whites until they are stiff but not dry. Add the second measure of sugar and beat until dissolved. Stir in the coconut and spread the mixture on top of the cake.

Bake in the preheated oven for 40–45 minutes or until a skewer inserted comes out clean. Be careful as the centre takes a long time to cook. Stand in the tin 10 minutes before turning out onto a cake rack to cool.

Store in an airtight container.

allyson's tip

Egg whites will gain greater volume if they are at room temperature before being whisked.

¾ cup caster sugar
50 grams butter, softened
1 egg, beaten
1½ cups flour
2 teaspoons baking powder
¾ cup milk

cinnamon & sugar topping
1 tablespoon butter, softened
2 tablespoons caster sugar
½ teaspoon cinnamon

mum's tea cake

makes 1 x 20-cm cake
preparation time **15 minutes**
cooking time **40 minutes**

This is still my favourite cake. My mother always made it when she was in a hurry to entertain friends. The flavour is simple from its basic ingredients and it is best served warm, cut in wedges and spread with a little butter.

Preheat the oven to 180 °C. Lightly grease and flour a 20-cm round cake tin.

Using a wooden spoon, mix together the sugar and butter. There is not enough to cream so mix as well as you can. Beat in the egg.

Sift the flour and baking powder together and fold into the butter mixture alternately with the milk.

Spoon the batter into the prepared cake tin.

Bake in the preheated oven for 40 minutes or until it is well risen, golden and the edge has shrunk from the side of the tin. Allow the cake to stand in the tin for 5 minutes before turning it out onto a cake rack. Do allow the cake to stand for 5 minutes before turning out of the tin as the freshly cooked cake will be too tender to turn out sooner and is likely to break in the process.

While the cake is still hot, spread the softened butter over the top and sprinkle over the sugar and cinnamon. Cut into 8–10 wedges and serve lightly buttered.

Mother is another name for love.
– Holly Hobby

375 grams butter, softened
2 cups caster sugar
2 teaspoons vanilla essence
grated rind of 1 large lemon
6 eggs, at room temperature
3½ cups flour
1½ teaspoons baking powder
1 teaspoon ground nutmeg
1 cup milk
2 cups currants, chopped raisins or
    dried cranberries

pound cake

makes 1 x 23-cm cake
preparation time **20 minutes**
cooking time **1 hour 20 minutes**

Moist and traditional, this wonderful cake has a flavour that improves on keeping. With its firm texture this is an ideal recipe to use for decorating.

Preheat the oven to 180 °C. Grease and line a 23-cm cake tin with baking paper.

Using an electric beater, beat the butter, sugar, vanilla essence and lemon rind together until smooth, light and creamy.

Add the eggs one at a time, beating well after each addition.

Sift the flour, baking powder and nutmeg together and gently stir one-third of the dry ingredients into the creamed mixture with a slotted spoon. Add one-third of the milk. Repeat with remaining dry ingredients and milk. Mix only until the ingredients are combined.

Stir in the dried fruit and turn into the prepared cake tin.

Bake in the preheated oven for 1 hour and 20 minutes, or until a skewer comes out clean.

Allow to cool in tin for 15–20 minutes before turning out onto a cake rack to cool.

Store in an airtight container for 3 days before cutting. This will allow the cake to set so that it cuts without crumbling and allow the flavours to marry.

250 grams butter, softened
1 cup sugar (caster is best)
grated rind of 2 lemons
4 eggs
1 cup plain unsweetened yoghurt
3 cups self-raising flour, sifted
½ cup semolina
410-gram can pear quarters in syrup,
    drained and juice reserved

pear syrup
reserved pear juice
¼ cup lemon juice
½ cup sugar

pear & semolina syrup cake

makes 1 x 23-cm cake
preparation time **20 minutes**
cooking time **1¼ hours**

This cake was a huge success on *Food In A Minute* and it remains a favourite in my home.

Preheat the oven to 180 °C. Grease and line a 23-cm round cake tin with baking paper.

In a large bowl, beat together the butter, sugar and lemon rind until light and fluffy.

Add the eggs one at a time, beating well after each addition. Stir in the yoghurt.

Fold in the flour and semolina. Transfer to the prepared cake tin.

Slice each pear quarter in half and arrange them on top of the cake.

Bake in the preheated oven for 1¼ hours until golden and a skewer inserted comes out clean.

Drizzle the pear syrup over the hot cake and set aside for at least 1 hour until cool. Serve lightly dusted with icing sugar in chunky wedges with a dollop of softly whipped cream.

pear syrup
While cooking the cake, prepare the syrup. Mix the reserved pear juice with the lemon juice and sugar in a small saucepan. Warm and stir regularly until the sugar has dissolved.

2 cups flour

1½ tablespoons balinese sweet spice mix

1 tablespoon baking powder

1½ cups molasses or muscovado sugar

½ cup desiccated coconut

150 grams butter, chilled and diced

1 cup coconut milk

1 egg

2 tablespoons vanilla essence

½ teaspoon baking soda

balinese sweet spice mix

2 teaspoons ground coriander

1 teaspoon ground cinnamon

2 teaspoons grated nutmeg

1 teaspoon ground cardamom

½ teaspoon ground cloves

casa luna spice cake

makes 1 x 20-cm cake
preparation time **20 minutes**
cooking time **1 hour**

Casa Luna is a delightful restaurant in Ubud, Bali. The owners, being Australian and Balinese, have created inspiring baking that reflect local flavours – this cake is served regularly.

Place the oven rack in the centre or just below centre of the oven. Preheat the oven to 170 °C. Lightly grease and line a 20-cm round cake tin with baking paper.

Sift the flour, spice mix and baking powder together into a large bowl. Stir through the sugar and coconut breaking up any large pieces of sugar.

Use fingertips to rub in the butter until the mixture resembles coarse crumbs.

Divide the mixture in half and press one half firmly into the base of the prepared cake tin.

Beat together the coconut milk, egg, vanilla essence and baking soda and stir into the remaining crumb mixture. Pour the batter into the prepared cake tin.

Sprinkle a little extra desiccated coconut on top, if wished, about 1–2 tablespoons.

Bake in the preheated oven for 1 hour or until a skewer inserted into the centre of the cake comes out clean.

Remove from the oven and stand for 15 minutes before turning out onto a cake rack to cool.

Serve slightly warm with whipped cream as a dessert or cold with freshly brewed coffee.

balinese sweet spice mix

Mix together the coriander, cinnamon, nutmeg, cardamom and cloves. Keep in an airtight container. Use with other coconut or tropical fruit dishes or baking.

75 grams butter, melted
1 cup sugar
2 eggs, beaten
2 tablespoons golden syrup
3 medium-sized apples, peeled and
    thinly sliced

2 cups flour
2 teaspoons baking soda
1 teaspoon ground nutmeg
2 teaspoons ground cinnamon
½ cup walnut halves

spiced apple & walnut cake

makes 1 x 20-cm cake
preparation time **20 minutes**
cooking time **45–50 minutes**

This moist cake is dense with apples and spices. Its flavour will vary depending on the variety of apples used.

Preheat the oven to 180 °C. Grease and line the base and sides of a 20-cm square cake tin.

In a large bowl, stir together the melted butter, sugar, beaten eggs and golden syrup.

Add the apple slices and toss to coat.

Sift the flour, baking soda, nutmeg and cinnamon together and stir into the apple mixture.

Turn into the prepared cake tin and place the walnut halves on top.

Bake in the preheated oven for 45–50 minutes, until a cake skewer inserted comes out clean. Cool in the tin for 10 minutes before turning out onto a cake rack. Dust with a thin layer of icing sugar, if wished, before serving warm with custard or cream.

Keep the cold cake in an airtight container and eat within 3–4 days.

variations

- Use pears and nashi in place of apples.
- Use half wholemeal and plain flour. The moistness of the apples works well with the coarser wholemeal flour.

2 large oranges, unpeeled
6 eggs
1 cup caster sugar
2 tablespoons lemon juice
1 teaspoon baking powder
3 cups ground almonds
about ¼ cup icing sugar to dust

orange almond cake

makes 1 x 23-cm cake
preparation time **3 hours**
cooking time **50–60 minutes**

This cake prepared from cooked oranges is incredibly moist with a slight bitterness that's a welcome change in a cake. I like it served warm, accompanied with a thick Greek-style yoghurt.

Place the unpeeled oranges into a saucepan. Cover with water and simmer for 1 hour. Drain and leave until thoroughly cold.

Preheat the oven to 180 °C. Grease and line a 23-cm cake tin with baking paper.

Cut the cooked oranges into quarters, remove the pips and place in a food processor fitted with a metal blade. Process until finely chopped. Add the eggs, sugar and lemon juice and process for 1 minute.

Add the baking powder and ground almonds and pulse only to mix. Do not over-process.

Pour into the prepared cake tin.

Bake in the preheated oven for 50–60 minutes until golden in colour and a cake skewer inserted comes out clean.

Stand in the tin for 10 minutes before turning out onto a cake rack to cool.

Sift over a thick layer of icing sugar. Heat 2–3 metal skewers over a gas flame and when red hot, drag through the icing sugar to make toffee stripes or a diamond pattern.

2 teaspoons instant coffee
    granules
1 cup hot water
¼ cup whisky or fruit juice
175 grams dark chocolate,
    chopped
250 grams butter, diced

1½ cups sugar
2 cups flour
1 teaspoon baking soda
2 eggs
1 teaspoon vanilla essence
1 quantity chocolate cream topping
    (see page 30)

mississippi mud cake

makes 1 x 23-cm cake
preparation time **40 minutes**
cooking time **1¼–1½ hours**

I have altered this recipe a little from my original baking book, cutting back the sugar and water and find this version more successful.

Preheat the oven to 140 °C. Grease and line a 23-cm cake tin with baking paper.

Put the coffee, hot water and whisky or fruit juice into a saucepan and bring to a simmer. Remove from the heat.

Add the chocolate and butter and stir until melted.

Add the sugar and stir until it has dissolved. Allow to cool.

In a large bowl, sift the flour and baking soda together and make a well in the centre.

Beat the eggs together with the vanilla essence and stir into the cooled chocolate mixture.

Pour the chocolate mixture into the dry ingredients and stir gently to mix.

Transfer to the prepared cake tin.

Bake in the preheated oven for 1¼–1½ hours until the cake has shrunk from the sides of the tin and is firm to the touch. Cool in the tin for 20 minutes before turning out onto a cake rack to cool.

Pour the warm chocolate cream topping over the cooked cake, spreading with a palette knife around the edges, if wished. Allow to stand for approximately 1 hour for the glaze to set before cutting into wedges.

Any remaining topping can be chilled and teaspoonful lots rolled into balls and used as decoration with cachous or similar.

Had I but a penny in the world,
thou shouldst have it for gingerbread.

– William Shakespeare

250 grams butter, diced
1 cup firmly packed molasses sugar
¾ cup whole milk
½ cup rum
½ cup good quality orange marmalade
2 eggs, beaten
grated rind of 2 lemons, oranges and
    limes
3 cups flour
2 teaspoons baking soda

1½ teaspoons baking powder
1½–2 tablespoons ground ginger
2 teaspoons ground cinnamon
1 teaspoon ground nutmeg
1 teaspoon ground cardamom
½ teaspoon ground cloves
150-gram packet crystallised ginger,
    finely sliced
¼ cup lemon and orange peel

barbados gingerbread cake

makes 1 x 23-cm cake
preparation time **30 minutes**
cooking time **1½ hours**

**Redolent with tropical spices, this is a moist gingerbread cake
that improves with keeping.**

Place the oven rack just below the centre of the oven. Preheat the
oven to 180 °C. Grease and line the base and sides of a 23-cm square
cake tin with baking paper.

In a saucepan, melt together the butter and molasses sugar, stirring
to make a smooth mixture of the two ingredients. Remove from the
heat and stir in the milk, rum, marmalade, beaten eggs and grated
citrus rinds. Set aside to cool.

Sift the flour, baking soda, baking powder, ginger, cinnamon, nutmeg,
cardamom and cloves together into a large bowl and make a well in
the centre.

Slowly pour in the cooled melted mixture, stirring to form a smooth
batter with almost all the crystallised ginger and all the peel.

Pour into the prepared cake tin. Sprinkle over the remaining
crystallised ginger.

Bake in the preheated oven for 1½ hours until well risen and firm to
the touch. Cool in the tin. This gingerbread tastes better if kept well
wrapped in an airtight container for two days before eating. Serve in
slices, buttered or unbuttered as wished.

allyson's tips

So Dark brown cane or muscovado
sugar can be used in place of
molasses sugar. For an even
lighter texture and flavour, use
soft brown sugar.

So If you do not have all the
spices, use the ginger and one
tablespoon mixed spice.

allyson's tip
Have the cream well-chilled to get the best volume and texture when whipping.

¼ cup cocoa
¾ cup milk
4 eggs, separated
½ cup caster sugar
300 ml cream
2 tablespoons icing sugar
1 teaspoon vanilla essence

squidgy chocolate roll

serves 10
preparation time 20 minutes
cooking time 25–30 minutes

This flourless chocolate Swiss roll is dense, chewy and moist.

Preheat the oven to 180 °C. Grease and line a standard 20-cm x 30-cm Swiss roll tin with baking paper.

Mix the cocoa and milk in a small saucepan and heat gently until the cocoa has dissolved. Set aside to cool thoroughly.

Using an electric beater, beat the egg yolks and sugar together until pale and fluffy. Beat in the cooled milk mixture.

In a scrupulously clean bowl, beat the egg whites with clean dry beaters until stiff but not dry. Fold into the cocoa mixture.

Quickly spread the mixture evenly into the prepared tin.

Bake in the preheated oven for 25–30 minutes until well risen and just firm to touch.

Working quickly turn out onto a sheet of clean baking paper, remove the baking paper lining and cover with a lightly damp tea towel. Leave to cool for 10 minutes before rolling up (in a clean tea towel) and leaving until cold.

Whip the cream, icing sugar and vanilla essence together. Unroll the sponge and spread the cream mixture over the sponge leaving a 1-cm edge at one of the shorter edges. From the opposite shorter side, roll up, enclosing the cream. Have the seam underneath.

Place on a long cake plate and dust with icing sugar before serving cut in thick slices.

150 grams butter, melted
¾ cup sugar
2 eggs, beaten
1 teaspoon vanilla essence
2 cups flour
2 teaspoons baking powder

½ teaspoon baking soda
½ cup milk
3 medium-sized bananas, mashed
1 quantity passion-fruit butter icing
    (see page 29)

banana cake

makes 1 x 20-cm cake
preparation time **30 minutes**
cooking time **35–40 minutes**

Banana cake is a Kiwi family favourite and this one with its no-creaming method is fast to make and tastes great.

Preheat the oven to 180 °C. Grease and line a 20-cm square cake tin with baking paper.

In a jug or small bowl, stir together the butter, sugar, beaten eggs and vanilla essence.

Sift the flour, baking powder and baking soda together into a large bowl and make a well in the centre.

Pour in the melted butter mixture and stir carefully with a wooden spoon, incorporating the milk and banana at the same time.

Turn the mixture into the prepared cake tin.

Bake in the preheated oven for 35–40 minutes or until a cake skewer inserted comes out clean.

Allow to stand in the tin for 10 minutes before turning out onto a cake rack to cool.

Ice with passion-fruit icing before serving in chunky slices.

2 cups wholemeal flour
¾ cup sugar (white or brown)
1 teaspoon baking powder
1 teaspoon baking soda
2 teaspoons ground nutmeg or mace
¼ cup oil
¼ cup milk
1 cup apple sauce

2 eggs
1 cup cold mashed pumpkin
10–12 juicy dried prunes, chopped

orange-scented cream cheese icing
125 grams cream cheese
3–4 tablespoons icing sugar
grated rind of 1 orange

pumpkin & prune cake

makes 1 x 20-cm cake
preparation time 30 minutes
cooking time 50–60 minutes

Sweet crown pumpkins make a wonderful cake that is even better spiked with dried fruits, like dates, figs, raisins, prunes or apricots.

Preheat the oven to 180 °C. Grease and line the base of a 20-cm ring cake tin with baking paper.

In a large bowl, stir together the wholemeal flour, sugar, baking powder, baking soda and nutmeg or mace. Make a well in the centre.

In a large jug or bowl, whisk together the oil, milk, apple sauce, eggs and pumpkin. Pour the wet ingredients into the dry and stir together gently with the prunes.

Turn into the prepared cake tin.

Bake in the preheated oven for 50–60 minutes until a cake skewer inserted comes out clean. Stand for 10 minutes before turning out to cool on a cake rack. Ice when cold.

orange-scented cream cheese icing
Beat together the cream cheese, icing sugar and orange rind.

allyson's tips

• Use a light-flavoured oil for this cake such as rice bran, canola, light olive or sunflower oil.

• Apple sauce can be bought, or to prepare it at home, cook 2 peeled and sliced apples in a little water. Drain and purée in a food processor until smooth. Pass through a sieve if wished.

• Vary the flavour by using cooked pears puréed to a sauce.

225 grams butter, softened
1 cup brown sugar
4 eggs, separated
grated rind of 1 orange
1 tablespoon lemon juice
1¼ cups self-raising flour
1 teaspoon baking powder
¾ cup ground almonds
¾ cup walnuts, chopped

2 cups grated carrots
1–2 pieces angelica, sliced, optional
1–2 glacé orange slices, optional

honey cream cheese icing
250 grams cream cheese
1 tablespoon manuka honey
lemon juice

carrot cake with honey cream cheese icing

makes 1 x 20-cm cake
preparation time **15 minutes**
cooking time **60–65 minutes**

At its height of culinary fashion in the early '80s, carrot cake was de rigueur for every new café bar. Take a trip back in time with this – leave the shoulder pads out though.

Preheat the oven to 180 °C. Grease and line a 20-cm cake tin with baking paper.

In a large bowl, beat the butter and sugar together until light and fluffy. Beat in the egg yolks, orange rind and lemon juice.

Sift the flour and baking powder together and stir through the ground almonds and walnuts.

In a clean bowl, beat the egg whites until stiff, but not dry, fold into the dry ingredients with the carrots. Gently stir the egg white mixture into the creamed mixture. Turn into the prepared cake tin.

Bake in the preheated oven for 60–65 minutes until golden brown and well risen and a skewer inserted in the centre comes out clean.

Leave in tin for 10 minutes before turning out onto a cake rack to cool. When cold, spread with honey cream cheese icing and decorate with angelica and small wedges of the glacé orange slices, if using.

honey cream cheese icing
Warm the cream cheese for about 20–30 seconds in the microwave. Beat until smooth. Add in the honey and sufficient lemon juice to make a spreadable mixture with a subtle sharp taste.

2 cups sultanas
150 grams butter, diced
1 cup sugar
2 eggs, beaten
2 cups flour
1 teaspoon baking powder

boiled sultana cake

makes 1 x 20-cm cake
preparation time 30 minutes
cooking time 1¼ hours

Every 1950s and 1960s community fundraising cookbook had a boiled fruit cake. They are simple and inexpensive to make and pretty fail-proof too. Jazz up this basic recipe with one of the ideas below.

Preheat the oven to 160 °C. Grease and line a 20-cm deep round cake tin.

Place the sultanas into a large saucepan, cover with water and bring to the boil. Simmer gently for 5 minutes then drain.

Add the butter to the hot sultanas and stir until melted. Stir in the sugar followed by the beaten eggs. Cool for 10 minutes.

Sift the flour and baking powder together and stir into the sultanas. Spoon into the prepared cake tin.

Bake in the preheated oven for 1¼ hours or until a skewer inserted comes out clean.

Cool in the tin for 30 minutes before turning out onto a cake rack to cool. Store in an airtight container for 2–3 days before cutting.

variations

- Add the grated rind of 1–2 oranges.
- Use mixed dried fruit or currants or raisins in place of sultanas.
- Add ½ cup chopped walnuts to the cake mix or use to decorate the top of the cake before baking.
- Use ½ honey and ½ sugar. Or use ¾ cup honey in place of the sugar.
- Use dark brown or muscovado sugar in place of white sugar.
- Simmer the fruit in ginger beer rather than water.
- Add 1–2 teaspoons mixed spice or apple spice mix (see page 18) or cinnamon or nutmeg.
- Use half wholemeal flour and half plain flour.
- Add ½ cup chocolate chips with the flour.

4 x size 7 eggs, at room temperature
¾ cup caster sugar
1 teaspoon vanilla essence
1¼ cups flour
1½ teaspoons baking powder
1 teaspoon butter, melted
3 tablespoons hot water

classic sponge cake

makes 1 x 20-cm cake
preparation time **20 minutes**
cooking time **25 minutes**

Have all the ingredients ready and measured before starting out to ensure a successful baked sponge.

Place the oven rack in the centre of the oven. Preheat the oven to 180 °C. Lightly grease a deep 20-cm round cake tin.

In an electric mixer, beat the eggs, sugar and vanilla essence with a pinch of salt until thick and creamy – about 10 minutes.

Working quickly, sift the flour and baking powder over the egg mixture. Use a slotted spoon to fold in, pouring the melted butter and hot water down the side of the bowl.

Quickly pour the mixture into the prepared cake tin.

Bake in the preheated oven for 25 minutes or until the sponge is elastic to the touch and shrinking from the sides of the tin.

Turn out at once onto a cake rack to cool completely.

When cold, use a serrated knife to cut the cake in half or three layers horizontally. Sandwich the layers with whipped cream, jam or lemon honey and top with whipped cream or a thick dusting of icing sugar.

allyson's tips

- The eggs will be thick and creamy when you can lift the beaters out of the mixture and draw a figure of 8 with the mixture that falls off the beaters. If you can still see the figure 8 when you have finished drawing then the mixture is thick enough.

- Use your hand to fold the flour, butter and hot water into the whipped egg mixture. Hands are more gentle and softer than a large spoon.

- Do not line the tins with paper or flour. Sponges have little fat and if the tins are protected with paper, the base and/or the sides of the sponges will have a moist, crustless appearance when the paper is removed. The exception to this is a Swiss roll.

- Do not stand a sponge in a draught when cooling as it will shrivel slightly.

If God had intended us to follow recipes,
he wouldn't have given us grandmothers.
– Linda Henley

200 grams butter, softened
1 cup caster sugar
3 eggs, at room temperature
1½ cups flour
2 teaspoons baking powder
¼ cup milk

½ cup raspberry jam (or use another favourite)
2–3 tablespoons icing sugar

victoria sponge

makes 1 x 20-cm cake
preparation time **15 minutes**
cooking time **20 minutes**

So named as it was a favourite of Britain's second longest reigning monarch Queen Victoria, 1837–1901, who enjoyed this simple yet elegant cake with tea.

Preheat the oven to 180 °C. Grease and line 2 x 20-cm round cake tins.

Beat the butter and sugar together until the mixture looks pale and fluffy.

Gradually beat in the eggs one at a time, beating well after each addition.

Sift together the flour and baking powder and fold into the creamed mixture alternately with the milk.

Divide the mixture between the prepared cake tins.

Bake in the preheated oven for 20 minutes or until a skewer inserted comes out clean. Stand for 2–3 minutes before turning out onto a cake rack to cool completely.

Spread the jam over the top of one of the sponge cakes. Place the remaining sponge cake on top and cover liberally with sifted icing sugar.

125 grams butter, softened
¾ cup caster sugar
1 teaspoon vanilla essence or
    grated rind of 1 lemon
2 eggs, at room temperature
2 cups flour
2 teaspoons baking powder
½ cup milk
¼ cup currants
2 tablespoons mixed peel

butter cake

makes 1 x 20-cm cake
preparation time 15 minutes
cooking time 40 minutes

A butter cake is a classic, plain, moist cake that can easily be creatively jazzed-up with many variations. Here I have added currants and mixed peel.

Preheat the oven to 180 °C. Grease and line a 20-cm round cake tin.

In a large bowl, beat the butter, sugar and vanilla essence or lemon rind until light and creamy. This can be done by hand or with electric beaters.

Add the eggs one at a time, beating well after each addition.

Sift the flour and baking powder together with a pinch of salt.

Fold into the creamed mixture alternately with the milk and dried fruit.

Transfer the mixture into the prepared cake tin.

Bake in the preheated oven for 40 minutes or until a cake skewer inserted in the centre of the cake comes out clean.

Stand in the tin for 10 minutes before turning out on a cake rack to cool. Ice if wished. Serve sliced and keep in an airtight container.

variations

- Omit the fruit and add the grated rind of 1–2 lemons or oranges.
- Use 1 cup finely chopped walnuts in place of the fruit.
- Make a marble cake. Omit the fruit, divide the cake into three portions and make each portion a different colour, e.g. pink, green and blue. Spoon the mixtures into the tin and swirl a knife through all the colours to marble them. Ice with a coloured butter icing.
- Omit the fruit and add grated rind of 1 lemon and ¼ cup poppy seeds.
- Omit the fruit and add ½ cup chocolate chips with the grated rind of 1 orange.
- Replace the currants with finely chopped glacé ginger or cherries.

allyson's tip

- Other tin sizes that can be used are:
  - 20-cm ring tin, cooking time around 35–40 minutes.
  - 2 x 23-cm sandwich tins or cake tins, cooking time around 25 minutes, join cakes with your favourite icing.
  - 23-cm x 10-cm loaf tin, cooking time 40–45 minutes.

allyson's tips

❧ Read the recipe before beginning, as you need to prepare the fruit the day before.

❧ Check that you have all the ingredients before starting.

❧ Prepare the cake tin before preparing the cake. The tin should be greased and lined with two layers of baking paper. The lining on the inside sides of the cake tin should extend above the top of the cake tin by 2 cm. The outside should be wrapped in 6–8 layers of newspaper and tied in place with heatproof string. This will protect the outside of the cake from over-browning.

❧ Old recipes call for the fruit to be washed and dried. This is not necessary today with the quality of dried fruit that we can purchase. However, it is still a good idea to wash glacé cherries and dry well to remove excess syrup.

❧ A rich fruit cake is very heavy and the mixture is stiff. This is to support the weight of fruit and nuts in the cake.

❧ As it takes time to make and cook a fruit cake, you can prepare it one day, cover with a loose cloth and bake it the next day.

❧ Make a shallow indent in the centre. This helps the cake to rise level on top when cooked.

500 grams raisins
500 grams sultanas
125 grams dried dates, chopped
150 grams glacé cherries, diced
150 grams mixed peel
150 grams sliced or flaked almonds

2 teaspoons ground mace or nutmeg
1 teaspoon mixed spice
½ teaspoon ground cinnamon or cloves
½ teaspoon ground white pepper
½ teaspoon salt

grated rind of 2 oranges
1 cup brandy
500 grams butter, softened
500 grams dark muscovado sugar
1 teaspoon vanilla essence
10 eggs, at room temperature

125 grams self-raising flour
500 grams flour
about 1 cup extra brandy, optional

traditional fruit cake

makes 1 x 25-cm cake
preparation time **overnight**
cooking time **3½–4 hours**

This is not an overly rich fruit cake. Though by cooking it with dark muscovado sugar you achieve a wonderful warm, mellow flavour. It is best made a month or two in advance to allow the cake to set – this ensures the cake will cut well.

Grease and line a deep-sided 25-cm square cake tin with two layers of baking paper. Make sure the paper has no creases and the corners are as sharp as possible to ensure square edges on the cake.

In a large bowl, put the raisins, sultanas, dates, cherries, mixed peel, almonds, mace or nutmeg, mixed spice, cinnamon or cloves, white pepper, salt, orange rind and brandy and toss together well. Cover and leave to macerate overnight.

Place the oven rack in the lower section of the oven, but not at the bottom. Preheat the oven to 160 °C.

With an electric mixer, beat the butter, sugar and vanilla essence until it is very light and creamy. Add the eggs one at a time, beating very well after each addition.

Sift the flours on top of the creamed mixture and then add the fruit and mix gently. Use your hands, it will be much easier and gentler on the fruit cake mixture.

Pack the mixture firmly into the prepared cake tin and level off the top evenly.

Wrap the outside of the tin in about 6–8 layers of newspapers, folding where necessary to make them look tidy. Secure with string.

Bake in the preheated oven for 3½–4 hours. If the cake begins to brown too much, cover with a sheet of baking paper and a thick covering of newspaper.

Place the cake on a board, cover with a clean tea towel and leave in the tin overnight to cool.

Sprinkle about ¼ cup extra brandy over the top of the cake. Remove from the tin, keeping the cake in the baking-paper lining and wrap in greased paper and then in foil. Over the next month, continue to pour the brandy in ¼ cup lots over the cake and re-wrap well after each time.

Decorate as wished with butter icing or a more classic marzipan and fondant icing.

This recipe will make 4–5 small (12-cm) cakes. Prepare the tins as above, but bake for 2–2½ hours. They are ideal Christmas gifts.

225 grams butter, preferably unsalted
1 cup caster sugar
4 eggs
½ cup flour
½ teaspoon baking powder
1½ cups ground almonds
200 grams marzipan

buttery marzipan cake

makes 1 x 20-cm cake
preparation time **15 minutes**
cooking time **50 minutes**

A layer of marzipan through this moist almond cake, makes it particularly special – especially if served warm with whipped cream. If you are not a fan of rich fruit Christmas cakes, this is an ideal substitute.

Preheat the oven to 180°C. Grease and line the base of a 20-cm square cake tin.

Beat the butter and sugar until the mixture is very light and fluffy. Add the eggs one at a time, beating well after each addition.

Sift the flour and baking powder together and mix with the ground almonds. Fold the dry ingredients gently into the creamed mixture.

Spread half the cake batter into the base of the prepared cake tin.

Roll the marzipan out on a bench lightly dusted with cornflour to a 19-cm square. Place on top of the cake batter.

Spread the remaining batter over the marzipan.

Bake in the preheated oven for 50 minutes, or until the cake is golden and has shrunk slightly from the sides of the tin.

Cool in the tin for 10 minutes before turning out onto a cake rack to cool thoroughly. When cold, wrap in foil and keep in an airtight container for 1-2 days before serving – if you have the time.

puds
& tarts

1½ cups self-raising flour
75 grams butter, diced
½ cup sugar
grated rind and juice of 1 orange
1 cup milk
1 cup blueberries, fresh or frozen and
    defrosted

sauce
boiling water
½ cup blueberry jam
½ cup sugar

self-saucing
blueberry pudding

serves 6
preparation time **15 minutes**
cooking time **45 minutes**

Preheat the oven to 180 °C. Lightly grease a 6-cup capacity ovenproof dish.

Sift the flour into a bowl. Rub in the butter until the mixture resembles fine crumbs.

Stir in the sugar and orange rind and make a well in the centre.

Pour in the milk, add the blueberries and mix with a slotted spoon to form a stiff batter.

Spread the batter into the prepared dish.

Make the orange juice up to 1½ cups with boiling water. Stir in the blueberry jam and sugar and pour over the batter.

Bake in the preheated oven for 45 minutes or until the sponge top is cooked in the centre.

Sprinkle with icing sugar before serving. Delicious accompanied with whipped cream.

variations
- Use raspberries and raspberry jam.
- Use diced fresh apricots and apricot jam.
- Use fresh boysenberries and boysenberry jam.
- Use diced peaches and marmalade.

1½ cups self-raising flour
2 tablespoons cocoa
½ cup sugar
1 cup milk
100 grams butter, melted
1 teaspoon vanilla essence

sauce
2 cups boiling water
½ cup sugar
2 tablespoons cocoa

family self-saucing chocolate pudding

serves 8
preparation time 15 minutes
cooking time 45 minutes

Preheat the oven to 180 °C. Lightly grease a 6-cup capacity ovenproof dish.

Sift flour and cocoa into a large bowl. Stir in the sugar and make a well in the centre.

Pour in the milk, butter and vanilla essence and mix quickly with a light hand using a slotted spoon to form a stiff mixture.

Spread the batter into the prepared dish.

Mix the boiling water, sugar and cocoa together and pour evenly over the batter.

Bake in the preheated oven for 45 minutes or until the sponge is cooked.

Serve hot dusted with icing sugar and accompanied with lashings of whipped cream, if wished.

Georgie Porgie pudding and pie
Kissed the girls and made them cry
When the boys came out to play
Georgie Porgie ran away.

allyson's tips

- A water bath is also called a bain marie. To make, sit the pudding in its dish in the centre of a large baking dish. Transfer to the oven and carefully pour cold water between the two dishes until the water comes half-way up the side of the dish holding the pudding. Take care when removing from the oven.

- This recipe can be easily doubled. Cook for 45–50 minutes. It will serve 6–8.

50 grams butter, softened
½ cup caster sugar
grated rind of 2 large lemons
2 eggs, separated
¼ cup flour, sifted
1 cup milk
¼ cup lemon juice

lemon delicious pudding

serves 4
preparation time **15 minutes**
cooking time **30–40 minutes**

I prefer this to any other self-saucing style pudding. Under the feathery light sponge top is a pool of golden lemon custard that beckons only for a little whipped cream to be served alongside.

Preheat the oven to 160 °C. Lightly grease a 3–4-cup capacity ovenproof dish.

Beat the butter, sugar, lemon rind and egg yolks together until light.

Gently stir in the flour, milk and lastly lemon juice.

Put the egg whites in a clean bowl and beat with an electric beater until they form stiff peaks but are not dry.

Fold the two mixtures together. Do not panic if the mixture looks curdled. Pour into the prepared dish.

Bake in the preheated oven for 30–40 minutes in a water bath until the top is golden and firm to the touch.

variation
- Use a mix of limes and lemons or try an orange version with 2–3 tablespoons of flaked almonds added.

3–4 cups stewed fruit
1 cup flour
1½ teaspoons baking powder
100 grams butter, softened
½ cup caster sugar
1 egg
½ cup milk

fruit sponge pudding

serves 6
preparation time 20 minutes
cooking time 30–35 minutes

Fruit sponges make a simple and tasty winter fruit pudding. Vary the pudding with whatever fruit is in season. I have listed some favourite fruit combinations at the end of this recipe.

Preheat the oven to 180 °C. Lightly grease a 6–8-cup capacity ovenproof dish.

Heat the fruit until very hot and place in the prepared dish. Keep in the preheated oven while making the sponge.

Sift the flour and baking powder together.

Beat the butter and sugar together until light and creamy.

Lightly beat the egg into the creamed mixture.

Fold the dry ingredients into the creamed mixture alternately with the milk. Spoon over the hot fruit.

Bake in the preheated oven for 30–35 minutes or until the sponge is well cooked and golden.

Sprinkle over sifted icing sugar. Serve hot with ice cream.

variations
Favourite fruit combinations:
- Rhubarb and raspberry with the grated rind of 1 orange.
- Pear or feijoas with 2 teaspoons of ginger added to the sponge.
- Apple with 1–2 teaspoons of mixed spice added to the sponge.
- Tamarillo and apple with 1 teaspoon of cinnamon added to the sponge.
- Pear sweetened with honey and spiked with the grated rind 1–2 lemons.
- Apple with the pulp of 2–3 passion-fruit.

The friendly cow, all red and white,
I love with all my heart;
She gives me cream with all her might,
To eat with apple-tart.
– Robert Louis Stevenson

125 grams butter, softened
2 cups flour
3 teaspoons baking powder
about 1 cup milk
about ½ cup jam

syrup
¾ cup boiling water
¾ cup sugar
75 grams butter, melted

grandma's jam roll

serves 6
preparation time **15 minutes**
cooking time **45 minutes**

Perhaps your grandmother made this sweet treat for a Sunday dinner. Perfect on a winter's eve with lashings of whipped cream.

Preheat the oven to 180 °C. Lightly grease a 6-cup capacity ovenproof dish.

Rub the butter into the flour and baking powder until the mixture resembles fine crumbs and make a well in the centre. Add sufficient milk to make a soft dough.

Turn out onto a lightly floured surface and just bring together.

With a floured rolling pin, roll the dough out to about 1-cm thickness. Spread the jam over the dough leaving a 1-cm edge all the way round free of jam. Roll up like a Swiss roll and place in the prepared dish.

Make the syrup by stirring together the water, sugar and butter and pour over the roll.

Bake in the preheated oven for about 45 minutes until the roll is golden and well risen. Serve sliced with a little of the sauce and custard or cream.

variations
- Use different jams.
- Sprinkle about ½ cup dried fruit over the jam before rolling up.
- Add the grated rind of 1 orange or lemon to the dough.

8 thick slices white bread
2–3 tablespoons butter, softened
1 litre milk
6 eggs
1 cup sugar (caster is good)
2 teaspoons vanilla essence

whisky sauce
1 cup sugar
2 tablespoons water
100 grams butter, softened
¼ cup whisky
2 eggs, beaten
¼–½ cup cream

bread & butter pudding with whisky sauce

serves 8–10
preparation time **20 minutes**
cooking time **1 hour**

The best bread to use for any bread and butter pudding is a firm white loaf with a hard crust or toast slice bread. The whisky sauce makes this family favourite a grown-up treat.

Preheat the oven to 180 °C. Lightly grease a large 8-cup capacity ovenproof dish.

Spread four slices of bread with the butter and make into sandwiches with the remaining four slices. Cut into chunks.

Place the bread in a large bowl and pour over the milk. Set aside.

Using an electric beater, beat the eggs, sugar and vanilla essence together until the mixture is quite thick and creamy. Pour into the soaked bread and stir well.

Transfer the mixture into the prepared baking dish.

Bake in the preheated oven in a water bath (see page 227) for 1 hour or until a knife inserted comes out clean. Stand for 10 minutes before serving warm with the whisky sauce.

whisky sauce
Put the sugar, water and butter into a small saucepan and heat gently, stirring constantly until the sugar has dissolved. Transfer the syrup to the top of a double saucepan and stir in the whisky and beaten eggs. Cook over mildly simmering water until the sauce has thickened. Stir in the cream.

*Honest bread is very well —
It's butter that makes the temptation.*
– Douglas Jerrold

1½ cups chopped dried dates
1 cup boiling water
2 teaspoons instant coffee
1 tablespoon vanilla essence
¾ teaspoon baking soda
175 grams butter, softened
1 cup brown sugar
3 eggs, beaten
1½ cups self-raising flour

sauce
125 grams butter
¾ cup brown sugar
¼ cup cream
¾ cup pecans or walnuts, chopped

toffee pecan pud

serves 6–8
preparation time 30 minutes
cooking time 30 minutes

Preheat the oven to 180 °C. Grease and flour a 23-cm ring tin.

In a large bowl, stir together the dates, water, coffee, vanilla essence and baking soda. Allow to stand for 10 minutes.

Beat the softened butter and sugar together until light and fluffy. Gradually beat in the eggs.

Carefully stir the flour into the creamed mixture with the date mix. The batter should be quite sloppy.

Pour the mixture into the prepared tin.

Bake in the preheated oven for 30 minutes or until a skewer inserted comes out clean. Stand in the tin while preparing the sauce.

For the sauce, put the butter, sugar, cream and pecans or walnuts into a saucepan and simmer together for 5 minutes.

Turn the pudding out onto a serving plate and serve in thick slices with plenty of sauce to accompany and scoops of vanilla ice cream.

3–4 tablespoons golden syrup
75 grams butter, softened
¾ cup caster sugar
2 eggs, beaten
1½ cups flour
2 teaspoons baking powder
¾ cup milk

golden syrup steamed pudding

serves 6–8
preparation time **20 minutes**
cooking time **1¼ hours**

This is my Mum's basic steamed pud recipe and it's a beaut! Serve with lashings of pouring cream and serve hot hot hot!

Put a trivet or an old saucer at the base of a deep saucepan and fill about one-third with water. Bring to the boil.

Grease the base and sides of a 5–6-cup capacity heatproof pudding bowl.

Spoon the golden syrup into the base of the prepared pudding bowl.

In a separate bowl, beat the butter and sugar until light and creamy. Add the beaten eggs gradually, beating well.

Sift together the flour and baking powder and fold into the creamed mixture alternately with the milk.

Spoon the batter on top of the golden syrup.

Cover with two layers of baking paper and one of foil and secure tightly with string.

Place the pudding into the saucepan of boiling water. The water should come about three-quarters of the way up the sides of the pudding bowl. Add more water from the kettle if required.

Cover with the saucepan lid and simmer away for 1¼ hours. Top up the water level with boiling water as it drops during cooking time.

Remove carefully from the heat. Stand 1–2 minutes before removing the foil and paper and turning out onto a plate to serve. If wished, spoon over extra golden syrup before serving.

to cook in the microwave
Grease the base and sides of a 5–6-cup capacity microwave-proof bowl. Spoon in 1 level tablespoon of the golden syrup. Fill with the pudding batter. Microwave uncovered on high power (100%) for 2 minutes, then cook on medium power (50%) for 10 minutes. Stand 1 minute before turning out onto a serving plate. Pour over the remaining golden syrup before serving. Tested in a 900w oven.

to cook in the oven
Grease a 20-cm cake tin and line with baking paper that comes halfway up the sides of the cake tin. Spread the golden syrup over the paper on the base. Top with the batter. Bake at 180 °C for 40 minutes or until a cake skewer inserted in the centre comes out clean. Stand 1–2 minutes before turning out upside down on a cake plate to serve.

Life is uncertain. Eat dessert first.

– Ernestine Ulmer

Now thrice welcome, Christmas,
Mince pies and plum porridge,
good ale and strong beer;
With pig, goose and capon,
the best that may be,
So well doth the weather
And our stomachs agree.

– Poor Robin's Almanack, 1695

¾ cup each whole almonds, walnuts and Brazil nuts

2 cups stale white breadcrumbs

1½ cups mixed dried fruit

¾ cup finely grated carrot

¾ dark brown or muscovado sugar

½ cup finely chopped prunes

½ cup finely diced dried figs

½ cup flour

125 grams Shreddo or butter, grated

½ cup Guinness or dark beer

4 eggs

2 tablespoons treacle or golden syrup, warmed

grated rind of 1 lemon and 1 orange

½ teaspoon each mixed spice and cardamom or ginger

classic hard brandy sauce

125 grams unsalted butter, softened

1–1½ cups sifted icing sugar

2–4 tablespoons brandy

guinness christmas pudding

serves 8–10
preparation time **1 hour**
cooking time **3 hours**

A classic pud recipe to share this Christmas. This pud can be cooked in a cloth or a bowl – both instructions are given here. In my house we accompany the pud with a classic hard brandy sauce and whipped cream.

Grease and flour the inside of a large oven roasting bag. Bring a very large pot of water to the boil with a trivet or old saucer in the bottom.

Finely chop the nuts and place in a large bowl with the breadcrumbs, dried fruit, grated carrot, sugar, prunes, figs, flour and Shreddo or butter. Stir together and make a well in the centre.

Beat together the Guinness or dark beer, eggs, treacle or golden syrup, citrus rinds and spices and pour into the well. Mix together well.

Pack the mixture into the prepared roasting bag and shape into a ball.

Wrap the ball in scalded calico and tie very securely with string to ensure the pudding remains water tight. Tie the ends of the calico together so that you can hook the hot pudding out at the end of cooking.

Place the pudding into the boiling water. Bring back to the boil, the water should cover the pudding.

Simmer the pudding gently for 3 hours, topping up with boiling water as the level gets low. Lift the pudding out and hang to dry suspended so that it forms a round cannonball shape. When cold and firm, store in the refrigerator.

bowl-cooked pud

Grease a 2-litre (8-cup) pudding bowl and pile the mixture into the bowl. Cover with 2 layers of baking paper, making a pleat in the centre to ensure room for the pud to rise if need be. Tie securely with string. Cover with a layer of foil, again with a pleat across the centre and tie with string. Cook as given above, ensuring that the water comes only three-quarters of the way up the sides of the pudding bowl. Top up with boiling water during cooking time. Store refrigerated.

to reheat for serving

Bring a large pot of water to the boil with the saucer in the base. Lower the pudding in. Simmer for 1 hour and then serve.

classic hard brandy sauce

Beat together butter, sugar and brandy. Serve slightly chilled.

coconut short pastry
1 cup flour
½ cup desiccated coconut
2 tablespoons caster sugar
100 grams butter, chilled and
  diced
about 3–4 tablespoons cold
  water

**chocolate & liqueur ganache
filling**
150 grams good quality dark
  chocolate, chopped
¾ cup cream
2 tablespoons brandy or
  Kahlua

petites tartes
au chocolat

makes 12–16
preparation time **40 minutes**
cooking time **12–15 minutes**

Oh, what decadence! For the craving chocoholic, this is truly heaven in a mouthful. Best accompaniments are coffee or liqueur.

Put the flour, coconut and sugar into a food processor and pulse to mix. Add the butter and process until the mixture resembles crumbs.

Pulse in sufficient cold water to form small moist balls of dough. Turn out onto a lightly floured surface to bring together.

Roll the pastry out to 3-mm thickness and use to line the base of 12–16 small tartlet tins. Use boat-shaped tins, patty-pan or mini muffin tins. Prick well with a fork. Refrigerate for 30 minutes.

Preheat the oven to 200 °C.

Bake in the preheated oven for 12–15 minutes or until the pastry is cooked. It will begin to turn toast coloured on the edges and the centre of the pastry should be cooked. Cool.

chocolate & liqueur ganache filling
Place the chocolate in a saucepan with the cream and stir over a low heat until the chocolate melts. Alternatively, heat on medium–high power in the microwave for about 5–6 minutes, stirring at regular intervals until the chocolate melts. Stir in the alcohol and set aside to cool completely.

When the chocolate mixture becomes thick but not set, spoon tablespoonfuls of the mixture into the prepared pastry cases. These are best served at room temperature.

allyson's tips

- For this ganache recipe look for a chocolate that has 60% cocoa solids or more. Check the back of the label when buying chocolate as the amount of cocoa solids is now listed as a percentage. The more cocoa solids, the darker the chocolate.

- The pastry cases can be cooked in advance and kept in an airtight container or even frozen and used as required.

- Any leftover ganache will keep for many weeks in an airtight container in the refrigerator.

- Galliano or an almond liqueur is also nice in this ganache recipe.

6 egg whites, at room
    temperature
¼ teaspoon cream of tartar
1 cup plus 2 tablespoons caster
    sugar
1 teaspoon cornflour
2 teaspoons vinegar
1 teaspoon vanilla essence

classic pavlova

serves 10
preparation time **20 minutes**
cooking time **1½ hours**

**This pavlova has less sugar in it than others and the
sugar is folded in not beaten, giving a rather denser
marshmallowy centre and chewier crust. It is my
favourite pavlova recipe of all.**

Place the oven rack in the middle of the oven. Preheat
the oven to 220 °C. Line a baking tray with baking paper
and mark out an 18-cm circle.

Place the egg whites and cream of tartar into a clean bowl
and beat with an electric beater until they form a dense
white foam and stiff peaks but the whites are not dry.

Sift the caster sugar and cornflour on top of the egg
whites and pour the vinegar and vanilla down the side of
the bowl. Use a slow speed to incorporate the ingredients
together. Do not beat and do not over-mix. Fold with a
slotted spoon in place of the beaters, if wished.

Spoon the mixture onto the prepared tray, spreading it
level with a spatula. The mixture will look very high,
which is okay as the pavlova expands when cooking.

Place into the preheated oven and immediately turn the
temperature down to 120 °C.

Bake for 1½ hours and then turn off the oven. Do not
open the oven door. Allow the pavlova to cool
thoroughly before removing.

The centre will crack and drop leaving a perfect hollow
for filling with whipped cream and topping with
seasonal fruits.

to bake in a tin
Pile the mixture into a well-greased and baking paper-
lined 23-cm spring-form cake tin. Bake as above.

pastry
2 cups flour
¾ cup pine nuts
½ cup caster sugar
100 grams butter, chilled and
    diced
3 egg yolks
3 tablespoons water

lemon custard
2 cups milk (or use 1 cup milk
    and 1 cup cream)
2 egg yolks
grated rind of 1 lemon
¼ cup cornflour
½ cup caster sugar
¾ cup pine nuts

pine nut custard tart

serves **8**
preparation time **1 hour**
cooking time **40 minutes**

Pine nuts, with their rich creamy flavour, are much loved by the Italians. Lemon has natural affinity with these tiny nuts, and the rich custard enclosed in a sweet short pastry makes an ideal dessert for special occasions.

Place the flour, pine nuts, sugar and butter in a food processor and process until the mixture looks like breadcrumbs.

Mix the egg yolks and water together and pulse into the crumb to form small moist balls of dough. Gather a little of the moist crumbs in your hand and if you can mould it together the mixture has had enough moisture added. Add extra water if needed, a tablespoon at a time.

Turn out onto a floured surface and bring together. Knead on a lightly floured bench for only about 1 minute. Wrap in plastic wrap and refrigerate for a minimum of 30 minutes while preparing the lemon custard.

Place 1¾ cups of the milk into a heavy-based saucepan and slowly bring to scalding point – just beneath boiling.

Mix the egg yolks, lemon rind, cornflour and sugar with the remaining milk. Quickly whisk into the hot milk and cook stirring constantly over a moderate heat until thick. Remove from the heat and set aside, covered, to cool completely.

Preheat the oven to 200 °C.

Roll the pastry out to 3-mm thickness and use to line the base and sides of a 24-cm loose-bottom flan tin. Trim off the excess and re-knead the pieces together. Set aside for decoration.

Fill the tart with the cold custard. Roll out the remaining pastry and cut into thin strips and use these to make a criss-cross pattern on top of the custard. Fill the diamond centres with pine nuts. If wished, brush the pastry strips with milk or beaten egg to glaze.

Bake in the preheated oven for 20 minutes and then lower the temperature to 180 °C for a further 20 minutes or until the pastry is cooked and golden. Allow to cool before serving dusted with icing sugar.

allyson's tip

❧ To cover a custard (or sauce), scrape any custard from the sides of the saucepan into the centre. Lightly butter a round of baking paper, large enough to cover the top of the custard, with an extra centimetre or two to come up the side of the saucepan. Place the paper greased-side down directly onto the custard. Set aside to cool. This way the custard (or sauce) will not form a skin on top. The paper will lift off easily.

½ cup sugar

1 soft vanilla pod, diced

200 grams dried nectarines, chopped

200 grams tropical dried fruit mix

100 grams butter, chilled and diced

¼ cup vanilla vodka or Galliano

1 quantity rich short pastry (see page 27)

75 grams marzipan

1 egg yolk

2 tablespoons water

vanilla fruit mince christmas tarts

makes 12 mini tarts
preparation time mince **30 minutes**, tart **30 minutes**
cooking time **18–20 minutes**

For the finest vanilla flavour, make this Christmas mince about one month in advance and keep refrigerated until required. They are a real treat and best enjoyed slightly warm and dusted with icing sugar.

In a food processor, place the sugar and vanilla pod until the vanilla is finely ground into the sugar.

Add the nectarines, fruit mix and butter and pulse to finely chop. Pour in the vodka or Galliano and pulse to mix. Store in a sealed glass jar in the refrigerator until required.

Roll out the pastry on a lightly floured bench to 3-mm thickness. Cut out 12 rounds to line 12 patty or small muffin tins. Knead the off-cuts of the pastry together and set aside. Cut 12 thin discs of marzipan and place in the base of each pastry-lined tin.

Spoon a large teaspoonful of mixture into each patty tin. Re-roll the remaining pastry and cut out 12 small discs or star shapes and place on top of the fruit mince. (You will use only half of the mince for this amount of pastry.)

Beat the egg yolk and water together and use to glaze the pastry tops. Refrigerate while preheating the oven to 180 °C.

Bake the tarts in the preheated oven for 18–20 minutes until golden and well-cooked.

Cool in the tins for 10 minutes before transferring to a cake rack to cool. Store in an airtight container. These tarts freeze well and can be easily reheated from frozen. Allow 15 minutes at 160 °C.

did you know?

❧ Christmas just wouldn't be the same without Christmas mincemeat pies. Nowadays 'mincemeat' is a spicy mix of dried fruits and chopped nuts. However, in medieval times – when the earliest type was identified – it was a small pastry called a 'chewette', containing chopped/shredded meat or liver, mixed with hard-boiled egg and ginger before being baked or fried. In later times the filling was enhanced with dried fruit, orange and lemon peel and sugar, which eventually usurped the meat altogether, to be replaced by suet. It was in the 16th century that such pies became associated with Christmas.

allyson's tips

➤ Make the breadcrumbs from day-old crusty bread. You can also use stale bread. Make crumbs in a food processor or rub pieces of bread between your hands. Stale bread crumbs easily.

➤ If the pie is prepared too far in advance of eating, the meringue topping will weep, leaving tiny pools of sugar syrup on top of the filling.

1 quantity basic sweet or rich
   short pastry (see page 27)

filling
1 cup fresh white breadcrumbs
2 cups cream
2 bay leaves, optional
2 teaspoons freshly grated
   lemon rind

¼ cup fresh lemon juice
¼ cup caster sugar
2–3 tablespoons brandy
6 egg yolks

meringue topping
6 egg whites
¾ cup caster sugar

lemon meringue pie

serves 8
preparation time 40 minutes
cooking time 40 minutes

This tart is a step back in time. It originated in Manchester, England, though initially it came without the glamorous meringue topping. That was added for the visit of Queen Victoria as the local, working-class dessert with its breadcrumbs was thought too humble. Like all meringue-topped pies, it needs to be eaten as soon as the meringue topping is cooked.

Preheat the oven to 190 °C.

Roll out the pastry on a lightly floured surface, large enough to cover the base and sides of a 24-cm round loose-bottom flan tin. If the sides are fluted, press the pastry into the sides firmly to ensure that on cooking, the tart has a highly patterned edge. Chill in the refrigerator for 30 minutes.

Line the pastry with baking paper and fill the centre with baking blind beans or material.

Bake in the preheated oven for 10 minutes. Remove the baking blind material and paper and continue to cook for a further 15 minutes or until the pastry is well cooked. Be careful that the edges of the sweet pastry do not over-brown.

In a saucepan, put the breadcrumbs, cream, bay leaves, if using, and lemon rind and bring to the boil. Reduce the heat and simmer gently for 5 minutes, stirring occasionally. Remove from the heat, discard the bay leaves and mix in the lemon juice, sugar and brandy.

Beat about 1 cup of the hot mixture quickly into the egg yolks. Once well incorporated, add this mixture to the saucepan and beat well. Pour the warm filling into the cooked pastry base.

Bake at 180 °C for about 20 minutes or until the custard has just set.

In a scrupulously clean bowl, whisk the egg whites until stiff but not dry. Beat in the caster sugar a little at a time, beating until all the sugar has dissolved and the meringue is thick and glossy. Spread the meringue over the top of the cooked filling.

Return the tart to a 220 °C oven for 5–10 minutes or until the meringue has set and the peaks of the meringue are just beginning to become golden. Serve quickly after cooking.

1 quantity basic short or rich short pastry (see pages 26 and 27)

filling
75 grams butter, softened
½ cup light muscovado or soft brown sugar

3 eggs
½ cup golden syrup
grated rind and juice of 1 large juicy lemon
¾ cup thread or desiccated coconut
¾–1 cup pine nuts, lightly toasted

golden syrup & pine nut tart

serves 8
preparation time **40 minutes**
cooking time **30–35 minutes**

This deliciously sweet tart is a variation on a pecan tart. A gorgeous smooth filling topped with buttery pine nuts is perfect for a special afternoon tea treat or a dessert.

Preheat the oven to 190 °C.

Roll out the pastry on a lightly floured surface and use to line the base and sides of a 20-cm round flan tin.

Bake blind in the preheated oven for 12–15 minutes. Remove the baking blind material and cook for a further 10 minutes or until the pastry is cooked in the centre.

In the food processor, process the butter, sugar, eggs, golden syrup, lemon rind and juice until smooth. Pulse in the coconut. Pour the mixture into the pastry case and sprinkle with the pine nuts.

Bake at 170 °C for 30–35 minutes or until golden and just set. Serve warm or cold with whipped cream, or a mix of yoghurt and whipped cream.

variations
- Use pecans or almonds in place of pine nuts.
- Use orange rind in place of lemon.
- Add 1 teaspoon ground ginger to the filling.
- Use maple syrup in place of golden syrup.

base
125 grams butter, softened
¾ cup sugar
2 eggs
1 teaspoon vanilla essence
¾ cup ground almonds
¾ cup flour
1 teaspoon baking powder
2 tablespoons cocoa, sifted

filling
¾ cup hazelnuts, toasted
75 grams chocolate, chopped
2 tablespoons sugar
1 tablespoon instant coffee
   granules

chocolate fudge & hazelnut tart

serves 8–10
preparation time **15 minutes**
cooking time **50 minutes**

This simply made tart is packed with chocolate flavour and can be made 2–3 days in advance before enjoying topped with whipped cream.

Preheat the oven to 180 °C . Grease and line the base of a 23-cm round loose-bottom tart or cake tin.

In a food processor, put the base ingredients – butter, sugar, eggs, vanilla essence, ground almonds, flour, baking powder – and process for one minute or until well mixed. Alternatively, beat together by hand.

Spread half the mixture onto the base and up the sides of the prepared tin.

To the remaining half, stir in the cocoa and set aside.

Into the food processor (there is no need to wash the bowl), put the filling ingredients – hazelnuts, chocolate, sugar and coffee granules and process until finely chopped. Alternatively, to prepare by hand, chop the nuts finely and grate the chocolate and mix with the sugar and coffee.

Sprinkle this mixture over the prepared base and carefully spread the chocolate cake mix on top.

Bake in the preheated oven 45–50 minutes until the centre is firm to the touch.

Cool in the tin for 10 minutes before turning out onto a cake plate to serve warm, dusted with icing sugar.

To serve cold, cool on a cake rack and spread with whipped cream and piped melted chocolate, if wished.

Families are like fudge —
most sweet with a few nuts.

– Author unknown

1 quantity rich short or basic sweet
   pastry (see page 27)

filling
2 eggs, lightly beaten
200 grams ricotta
50 grams butter, melted and cooled
2 tablespoons brandy

2 tablespoons caster sugar
¼ teaspoon ground nutmeg
¾ cup ground almonds
grated rind and juice of 1 large
   juicy lemon
2 tablespoons currants
2–3 tablespoons slivered almonds

maid of honour tarts

makes 12 tarts
preparation time 40 minutes
cooking time 20 minutes

One legend recalls that these tarts were favourites of Ann Boleyn when she was maid of honour to Catherine of Aragon at Hampton Palace. Another recalls that tarts similar to these were fare of the wealthy who circulated around Kew and so another name recorded for them is Richmond Tarts. Wherever they hail from, these delicious sweet tarts are the perfect treat for a special occasion like Mother's Day.

Preheat the oven to 200 °C.

Roll the pastry out on a lightly floured surface to about 3-mm thickness and cut out rounds and use to line patty-pan tins. There should be sufficient to line 12–16 depending on the size of the patty-pan tins. Chill in the refrigerator while making the filling.

Beat together the lightly beaten eggs, ricotta, butter, brandy, sugar and nutmeg. Stir in the ground almonds, lemon rind, juice and currants and mix well.

Divide the mixture evenly among the pastry tarts. Sprinkle a few slivered almonds on top.

Bake the tarts in the preheated oven for 20 minutes or until golden and the filling is firm to the touch.

Serve warm and, if wished, sprinkled with icing sugar and a little cinnamon.

250 grams butter, softened
¾ cup caster sugar
1 egg
grated rind of 1 orange
1 teaspoon vanilla essence
2½ cups flour
2½ teaspoons baking powder
400-gram can dark plums in syrup,
    well drained
icing sugar to dust

no-fuss plum tart

serves 8
preparation time 15 minutes
cooking time 40 minutes

My all-time favourite recipe from the many years I presented *Food in a Minute*.

Preheat the oven to 190 °C. Lightly grease and flour a 23-cm round cake tin.

In a bowl or food processor, mix together the butter, sugar, egg, orange rind and vanilla essence until well mixed.

Add the flour and baking powder and stir or pulse to mix in.

Press two-thirds of the mixture onto the base of the prepared tin.

Halve and stone the plums. Arrange over the base.

With floured hands dot the remaining dough on the top.

Bake in the preheated oven for 40 minutes. Stand 10 minutes before serving dusted with icing sugar and accompanied with lashings of whipped cream.

variations
- Use canned apples and lemon rind.
- Use poached or stewed rhubarb.
- Use 1½–2 cups fresh raspberries.

fast & furious

variations

raspberry & hazelnut shortcakes

➤ Use toasted blanched and finely chopped almonds and add a few drops of almond essence to the pastry when kneading. Perfect with raspberries.

➤ Use finely chopped pistachio nuts and add the grated rind of a lemon. Delicious with blackberries.

➤ Use toasted and finely chopped macadamia nuts and dip or decorate the top biscuit with melted chocolate. Lovely with blueberries.

pear & ginger hearts
raspberry & hazelnut shortcakes

½ cup hazelnuts, toasted
400-gram packet frozen sweet
    short pastry, defrosted
½ cup cream, thickly whipped
½ cup fruit yoghurt
250 grams raspberries, fresh
    or frozen and defrosted or 1
    punnet strawberries

2 sheets frozen puff pastry,
    defrosted
beaten egg or milk to glaze
2 tablespoons finely chopped
    crystallised ginger
410-gram can pear quarters,
    well drained

2 tablespoons your favourite
    honey
2 tablespoons finely chopped
    pistachio nuts, optional

raspberry & hazelnut shortcakes

serves 4
preparation time 15 minutes
cooking time 12–15 minutes

This dessert yells more dash than cash at you.

Preheat the oven to 180 °C. Lightly grease a baking tray or line with baking paper.

Rub the toasted and cooled hazelnuts in your hands over the sink to allow the papery skins to fall away. Chop very finely.

On a lightly floured bench knead the pastry and hazelnuts together.

Roll the pastry out to 3–4-mm thickness and cut out 8 x 8-cm wide heart shapes or other shapes. Place the shapes on the prepared tray.

Bake in the preheated oven for 12–15 minutes until golden. Transfer to a cake rack to cool.

Gently stir together the whipped cream and yoghurt and sweeten to taste as wished.

To serve, pile one biscuit with cream and top with raspberries or strawberries. Sprinkle the second biscuit well with icing sugar and serve on top. Garnish as wished.

Repeat with remaining biscuits, cream and fruit. Serve within 30 minutes of decorating.

pear & ginger hearts

serves 4
preparation time 10 minutes
cooking time 12–15 minutes

These simple individual fruit tarts are a regular on my menus and can be varied so easily to suit whatever is in the pantry.

Preheat the oven to 220 °C. Lightly grease a baking tray or line with baking paper.

Cut the pastry sheets into 8 x 8–10-cm rounds or 8-cm heart shapes and place on the prepared trays. Prick the pastry shapes with a fork and chill for 10 minutes.

Brush the pastry rounds with the beaten egg or milk and then arrange equal amounts of ginger on each shape in the centre. Top each with 2 pear quarters and glaze the pears with a little honey.

Bake towards the top of the preheated oven for 12–15 minutes until golden.

If wished, brush with more honey and decorate with pistachio nuts, if using, and a dusting of icing sugar before serving warm.

variations
- Use chopped chocolate in place of the ginger.
- Use canned apricots, peaches or plums.
- Use fresh poached fruit scented with spices or poached in wine for a more chic recipe.

½ cup merlot
¼ cup sugar
pared rind of 1 orange or lemon
1 punnet strawberries, hulled and
   sliced
250 grams chilled cheesecake filling
   mix or mascarpone
½ cup custard, chilled
12 mini sweet pastry tartlet shells

merlot strawberry tartlets

makes 12
preparation time **15 minutes**

A little on the rich side, but ever so easy and delicious.

Simmer merlot, sugar and orange or lemon rind together for 5 minutes. Cool. Add the strawberries and marinate for a few minutes.

Beat the chilled cheesecake filling or mascarpone and custard together until smooth. Spoon the filling into the tarts evenly.

Drain and arrange the strawberries on top and serve any remaining merlot mix alongside.

Serve soon after decorating.

quick peach tart

½ x 350-gram packet plain butter cake mix
½ cup desiccated coconut
75 grams butter, melted
1 egg, beaten
grated rind of 1 orange
2 tablespoons orange juice

peach cream filling
410-gram can peaches, well drained
250-gram pottle sour cream
1 egg
2 tablespoons orange juice

½ cup cream
125 grams dark chocolate
24 mini pre-made meringue nests

quick peach tart

serves 6–8
preparation time **15 minutes**
cooking time **35–40 minutes**

This is so simple and delicious and it's so quick because it uses that emergency pack of cake mix hiding away in the back of the pantry!

Preheat the oven to 180 °C. Grease and line a shallow-sided 20-cm round cake tin.

Stir together the cake mix, coconut, melted butter, egg, orange rind and juice to form a dough.

Press into the prepared tin, bringing the mix up the sides of the tin.

Arrange sliced peaches over the base.

With a fork, beat together the sour cream, egg and orange juice and pour on top of peaches.

Bake in the preheated oven for 35–40 minutes or until the cake mix is golden around the edges and the filling set.

Serve dusted with cinnamon and/or icing sugar.

chocolate meringue nests

makes 24 meringues
preparation time **30 minutes**

Add these to a fruit platter for a quick, easy dessert with style.

Put the cream and chocolate into a microwave-proof bowl. Heat on high power (100%) for 2 minutes. Stir to make the chocolate a smooth sauce.

Refrigerate until thick.

Fill or pipe the thick chocolate cream (ganache) into the centre of the meringue nests.

Dust with icing sugar, if wished, before serving.

variation
❧ Use the filling to join 2 small meringues together.

Pictured overleaf.

200 grams pre-made
  Christmas pudding
¼ cup mini chocolate chips

2 tablespoons whisky, rum or
  brandy
100 grams dark chocolate,
  melted

1 cup macadamia nuts
1 cup hazelnuts
2–3 mini meringues, coarsely
  crushed
200 grams white chocolate,
  chopped

250 grams dark chocolate,
  chopped
few drops essential orange oil,
  optional

mini chocolate christmas pudding truffles

makes 20
preparation time **10 minutes**
chilling time **1 hour**

These delectable little treats were an absolute hit on our photography shoot day. They are so simple to make yet taste so delicious – making truffles has never been easier.

Crumble the pudding into a bowl and toss through the chocolate chips and whisky, rum or brandy. Mix well and shape half tablespoonful lots into small balls. Refrigerate for 1 hour.

Melt the dark chocolate in the microwave on high power (100%) for about 2 minutes or until almost all the chocolate has melted. Remove, stirring until all the chocolate has melted and become smooth.

Using a fork or spoon, dip the balls into the chocolate to cover and allow the excess chocolate to fall off before placing onto a paper-lined tray. Allow the chocolate to set.

When set remove carefully and transfer to a lidded container. Keep refrigerated or in a very cool place. If wished, decorate with cachous or drizzle with melted white chocolate.

hazelnut & meringue brittle

serves 12–16
preparation time **20 minutes**
chilling time **2 hours**

This is a quick and easy-to-make chocolate treat to serve with coffee. If you do not have the orange oil, use the grated rind of an orange.

Preheat the oven to 180 °C. Line a 20-cm x 30-cm Swiss roll tin with baking paper.

Toast the macadamia nuts and hazelnuts for 8 minutes or until golden in colour. The macadamia nuts, being larger, may take a little longer than the hazelnuts; allow about 10 minutes.

Allow the nuts to cool. Rub the hazelnuts in a tea towel or in your hands over a sink to remove the skins.

Chop the nuts roughly and scatter over the prepared tin and scatter the crushed meringue on top.

Melt the chocolates in separate bowls by placing in the microwave on high power (100%) for about 2 minutes, stirring occasionally. Scent the dark chocolate with orange oil, if using.

Pour the two chocolates over the nuts and meringue mixture and, if wished, shake to make a swirly pattern.

Refrigerate for 2 hours or until the chocolate has set. Break into pieces to serve.

allyson's tips

hazelnut & meringue brittle
- Use the pre-bought meringues. Store any leftovers in an airtight container. They are ideal to serve with fruit and cream for a quick summer-time dessert.

- Do not use orange essence as this will cause the chocolate to sieze.

truffles
- Use store-bought Christmas pudding – it's quick and easy to use. Or use leftover Christmas pudding or cake.

- In place of alcohol, use fruit juice.

chocolate meringue nests (page 265)
mini chocolate christmas pudding truffles
hazelnut & meringue brittle

½ cup hazelnuts

2 sheets frozen pre-rolled puff pastry, defrosted

50 grams butter, softened

¼ cup brown sugar

1 egg, beaten

2 cups cake crumbs or use fresh white breadcrumbs

¼ cup sultanas, currants or raisins

grated rind of 1 orange or lemon, or 1 teaspoon mixed spice

milk to glaze

hazelnut & fruit roll

serves 6–8
preparation time **30 minutes**
cooking time **30–35 minutes**

Vary this recipe with different styles of crumbs, try coconut or chocolate cake crumbs, or use white or fruit breadcrumbs, or whatever is to hand.

Preheat the oven to 200 °C. Lightly grease a baking tray.

Toast the hazelnuts on a separate tray for 5–7 minutes or until just golden. Cool. Rub between your hands over a sink to allow the skins to fall away. Chop the nuts finely.

Place the 2 sheets of pastry on top of each other on a lightly floured bench. Roll out to a 40-cm x 25-cm rectangle. Leave to rest while preparing the filling.

Mix the butter and sugar together and work in the egg a little at a time. Stir in the crumbs, dried fruit, nuts and rind or spice.

Spread the cake mixture over the pastry, leaving a 0.5-cm edge free of the filling around the entire rectangle. Brush this edge with milk.

Roll up from the longer edge like a Swiss roll, finishing with the join underneath.

Place on the prepared tray and join the edges together to make a circle. Brush with more milk to glaze and sprinkle with a little caster sugar, if wished. Make slits in the pastry with a sharp knife.

Bake in the preheated oven for 30–35 minutes until well risen and golden. Cool for 10 minutes before serving hot with whipped cream and ice cream.

2 sheets frozen pre-rolled puff
    pastry, defrosted
milk or egg wash to glaze
300-ml bottle cream
2 tablespoons icing sugar
dash vanilla essence

cream horns

makes 12
preparation time 15 minutes
cooking time 15 minutes

Once the realm of every good tea party in the '60s and '70s, cream horns are incredibly easy to make and they look great. Fill with fruit or mousse, if wished.

Preheat the oven to 220 °C. Lightly grease 1–2 baking trays or line with baking paper. Lightly grease 12 cream horn moulds.

Brush the pastry sheets with milk or egg wash to glaze. Using a wetted cook's knife, and using a definite sharp action, cut the pastry sheets into 1.5-cm wide strips. Do not drag the knife through the pastry as the edges will not puff up.

Holding the cream horn moulds in one hand, begin to wrap the pastry strips around the moulds, starting at the base. Overlap the strips a little each time and make sure the pastry does not over-hang on the end of the mould. You will need more than one pastry strip to complete each mould.

Place on the prepared baking tray and repeat with the remaining pastry.

Bake in the preheated oven for 15 minutes or until golden and the pastry is well cooked. Cool for 5 minutes before carefully removing the pastry horns from the moulds. Do not leave until cold as the pastry will stick to the moulds. Allow to cool completely on a cake rack.

Whip the cream, sugar and vanilla essence together until firmly whipped and use to fill the cream horns. Dust with icing sugar before serving.

filling variations
- Flavour the cream with 2 tablespoons of your favourite liqueur or spirit.
- Add the grated rind of a lemon or orange to the cream.
- Flavour the cream with almond or lemon essence or rosewater.
- Add chocolate hail to the cream.
- Mix half whipped cream and mascarpone together for a very rich alternative.
- Fill the bases with fresh berries or fresh berries marinated in a little liqueur.
- Fill the ends with melted chocolate and fill with whipped cream or mousse.

yeast

¼ cup sugar
½ cup warm water
2½ teaspoons Surebake yeast mix
50 grams butter, melted
1¾ cups flour, sifted
1 egg
½ teaspoon salt

hazelnut topping
½ cup chopped hazelnuts
¼ cup brown sugar
¼ cup fresh white breadcrumbs
2 tablespoons chopped crystallised ginger
2 tablespoons mixed peel, optional
50 grams butter, melted

hazelnut coffee cake

serves 8
preparation time 1½ hours
cooking time 40–45 minutes

This is a simple yeast-based cake, best served with a morning coffee.

Grease a 23-cm round cake tin.

In a large bowl, stir together the sugar, warm water and yeast. Stand for 10–15 minutes until the mixture is frothy.

Stir the butter and half the flour into the liquid ingredients.

Beat in the egg and, once incorporated, add the remaining flour and salt.

Spread into the prepared cake tin. The dough will be quite sticky and is best pushed into the tin with floured or damp fingers.

Scatter the topping over the dough and set in a warm place for about 60 minutes or until double in bulk.

Preheat the oven to 190 °C.

Bake for about 40–45 minutes or until well risen, golden and shrunk from the sides. Stand in the tin for 5 minutes before turning out to serve.

hazelnut topping
Stir together the hazelnuts, sugar, breadcrumbs, ginger, mixed peel, if using, and butter.

variations
- Use macadamias or almonds in place of hazelnuts.
- For an extra crunchy topping, use demerara sugar in place of brown sugar.

allyson's tip

❧ In a cool kitchen, this dough may take an extra 15 minutes to rise. If your kitchen is cool, or even if it is winter time, wrap the tin in a warmed bath towel or several warmed tea towels and place in an area where there are no cool draughts.

did you know?

❧ Coffee cake in America refers to a simple, sweet, yeast-based cake served with morning coffee.

Back: pizza bread with olive oil and rosemary
Centre: pizza bread with feta, garlic and rosemary
Front: pizza bread with parsley and Parmesan

1½ cups warm water
2 teaspoons active dry yeast
½ teaspoon sugar
500 grams high grade flour
1 teaspoon salt
3 tablespoons olive oil

basic pizza dough

makes 2 large pizzas
preparation time 1¼ hours
cooking time 10–12 minutes

Use a food processor to make this dough in a jiffy. It is the only pizza dough recipe I use.

Put the warm water in a large 3-cup capacity jug and sprinkle in the yeast and sugar. Stir to mix well and set aside for about 5–8 minutes until the yeast has dissolved and has become soft and spongy on top of the water.

Put the flour and salt into a food processor and with the motor running pour in the frothy yeast mixture and olive oil as fast as the flour can absorb it.

Process the dough for 1 minute or until the dough forms a ball that rides around the blade in the machine and does not cling to the bowl. Add a little more flour or water if required.

Transfer the dough to a lightly greased bowl, cover with plastic wrap and set aside for about 45 minutes until it is double in bulk.

Place the oven rack towards the top of the oven. Preheat the oven to 230 °C. Preheat a pizza stone, if using, or grease or dust with flour an oven tray.

While the dough is proving prepare any toppings.

Turn the dough out onto a floured bench and divide in half. Roll one portion out to about 26–28-cm and working quickly roll the dough around a rolling pin and unroll onto the hot pizza stone or oven tray. Brush liberally with oil and scatter over any toppings, if using.

Bake in the preheated oven for 10–12 minutes or until the pizza base is golden and the toppings hot. Repeat with the remaining dough.

topping ideas
- Olive oil or lemon-scented olive oil and flaky salt.
- Olive oil and rosemary leaves.
- Olive oil, crumbled feta, sliced garlic and rosemary leaves.

variation
- Knead ¼–½ cup finely chopped parsley and ¼ cup grated Parmesan into the dough before leaving to rise and double in bulk.

ferment
1 egg
1 cup water
3½ teaspoons active dry yeast
1 cup high grade flour
1 teaspoon sugar

dough
2½ cups high grade flour
¼ cup sugar
1 teaspoon salt
50 grams butter, softened

fruit & spice filling
75 grams butter, softened
¾ cup currants or sultanas
1½ teaspoons ground cassia or
    cinnamon
grated rind of 1 orange
¼ cup mixed peel

chelsea buns

makes 12 buns
preparation time **3 hours**
cooking time **15–20 minutes**

ferment

In a medium jug, use a fork to beat together the egg, water, yeast, flour and sugar. Set aside for 10–12 minutes or until the mixture is bubbly and frothy. On cooler days this may take a little longer.

dough

Sift the flour, sugar and salt into a large bowl and make a well in the centre. Pour in the bubbling ferment and use your hand to bring the dough together. Add the softened butter towards the end. It may be necessary to add 2–3 tablespoons extra water or milk to make a soft dough.

Turn the dough out onto a lightly floured surface and knead for a good 10 minutes until the dough is smooth. Turn the dough over in a clean greased bowl and cover with plastic wrap and a warmed towel and sit in a warm place for 40 minutes or until double in bulk.

Turn the dough out onto a lightly floured surface and flatten gently to deflate the dough. Do not knock down roughly.

Roll out to a 36-cm x 30-cm rectangle. Spread generously with the 75 grams softened butter for the filling. Toss together the remaining fruit and spice filling ingredients and scatter over the buttered dough. Roll up from the longer edge as tightly as you can.

Cut into 12 x 3-cm thick slices and place the slices into a well-greased and lined 25-cm square cake tin or baking dish. Cover and leave for 40 minutes until double in bulk. Preheat the oven to 220 °C while the dough is rising.

Place into the preheated oven and immediately lower the temperature to 200 °C. Bake for 15–20 minutes or until the buns are golden and the dough is well cooked.

Remove from the oven and brush either with a little butter or for a sweeter finish a little sugar syrup. Cool in the tin for 5 minutes before turning out and serving warm with butter.

simple sugar syrup

Stir together equal quantities of sugar and water over a low heat until the sugar has been dissolved. Keep refrigerated. For the buns, you will need about 2–3 tablespoons sugar syrup to brush over.

filling variations

- Dried cranberries, orange rind, cassia and mixed peel.
- Chopped fresh dates, lemon rind, cinnamon and chopped glacé ginger.
- Dried blueberries with orange rind, cinnamon or mace and mixed peel.

allyson's tip

❧ Many elements affect the amount of liquid needed to make a soft dough. Age of the flour, accurate measuring, dryness of the flour, size of the egg, etc. It is worthwhile remembering that the softer the dough, the better the end result.

did you know?

❧ Originally, a favourite at the Bun House in Chelsea, which was frequented by royals and Britain's upper class. This rich yeast bun has become a firm favourite in many countries and now that there is a greater variety of dried fruits, you can make any number of flavour variations (see opposite).

There's charm in the sound, which nobody shuns of smoking hot, piping hot, Chelsea buns.

1½ teaspoons active dry yeast
or 1½ tablespoons Surebake
yeast mix
1 cup warm milk
100 grams butter, softened
2 eggs
4 cups high grade flour

1 teaspoon salt
½ teaspoon each ground
allspice, mixed spice,
cinnamon and nutmeg
¼ cup brown sugar
1 cup mixed dried fruit
milk or egg wash to glaze

cross paste
½ cup flour
¼ teaspoon baking powder
1 tablespoon butter
about ¼ cup milk

classic hot cross buns

makes 16
preparation time **3 hours**
cooking time **20–25 minutes**

Home-made hot cross buns are wonderful when enjoyed with family and friends at Easter.

Lightly grease a baking tray or line with baking paper.

Stir the yeast and milk together and set aside in a warm place for 15 minutes or until the mixture is frothy.

Beat softened butter and eggs into the frothy mixture.

Put the flour, salt, spices and brown sugar into a food processor and pulse to sift.

Turn the food processor on. Pour the yeast mixture slowly down the feed tube until it forms a soft dough. Process for 1 minute. Add the dried fruit and pulse to just mix.

Turn the dough into a greased bowl, turn over and cover with greased plastic wrap. Set aside in a warm place for about 1 hour until the dough has doubled in bulk.

Turn out onto a lightly floured surface and divide into 16 equal portions. Shape each portion into a ball and place on the prepared tray with about 1-cm space between each bun.

Cover with a lightweight clean tea towel and set aside in a warm place for about 30 minutes until well risen.

Place the oven rack in the centre of the oven. Preheat the oven to 190 °C.

Brush the buns with milk or egg wash to glaze. Pipe thin crosses onto the buns with the cross paste.

Bake in the preheated oven for about 20–25 minutes.

Brush the hot buns with the sugar glaze (below) and return to the oven for 1 minute. Remove from the oven and transfer to a cake rack to cool.

cross paste
Sift flour and baking powder together. Rub in butter. Stir in enough milk to make a thick batter that can be piped.

sugar glaze
Dissolve 2 tablespoons sugar in 2 tablespoons hot milk.

making by hand
Sponge the yeast as outlined in steps 2 and 3. Sift the flour, salt, spices and brown sugar into a large bowl and stir through the dried fruit. Make a well in the centre. Gradually mix in the frothy yeast mixture. Once most of the flour has been absorbed, turn the dough out onto a lightly floured bench and knead well for 10 minutes until the dough is smooth. Continue as above.

allyson's tip

❧ Savarin tins are smooth, shallow and seamless. Once the dough is cooked, it is saturated in a sweet syrup, so, if you use a loose-bottom ring tin, stand the tin in a shallow dish to catch any syrup that may seep through the join.

did you know?

❧ Kirsch, or correctly named Kirschwasser, is cherry brandy and it originated in Germany, where the cultivation of cherries was once centred around the Black Forest region. Black Forest gateau, the well-known chocolate sponge cake layered with cherries and cream and flavoured with Kirsch, originated in this area.

¾ cup milk, warm
1 tablespoon sugar
1 teaspoon active dry yeast or 1
    tablespoon Surebake yeast
    mix
2 cups flour
1 teaspoon salt
4 eggs, lightly beaten
125 grams butter, melted

syrup
1¾ cups caster sugar
2 cups water
1 teaspoon vanilla essence
½ cup Kirsch, or your favourite
    liqueur or fruit juice

filling
300 ml cream
icing sugar to sweeten
2 punnets fresh strawberries or
    a mix of summer berries

savarin

serves 10
preparation time 1½ hours
cooking time 25–30 minutes

Yeast is the essential ingredient in this rich and buttery ring cake. Savarin is a European favourite, drenched in Kirsch-flavoured syrup and served with plenty of fresh fruit and cream. It's usually a time-consuming recipe, however, this version is much simpler and tastes just as delicious.

Grease and lightly flour a 23-cm savarin or ring tin.

Stir the milk, sugar and yeast together and set aside for 10–15 minutes or until the yeast becomes very frothy.

Sift the flour and salt into a large bowl and make a well in the centre.

Pour in the frothy yeast mixture and the lightly beaten eggs.

Using your hands, blend the ingredients into a batter. Beat with your hand for 10 minutes or until the batter is shiny.

Add the butter and beat well for 3–4 minutes.

Pour the batter into the prepared savarin or ring tin. Cover with a clean light cloth. Set aside in a warm place for about 1 hour until the batter has doubled in bulk.

Place the oven rack in the centre of the oven. Preheat the oven to 190 °C. Prepare the syrup and leave it to cool.

Once the batter has doubled in bulk, bake in the preheated oven for 25–30 minutes or until well risen, golden and firm to the touch.

Remove from the oven and allow the savarin to stand in the cake tin for 5 minutes. Pierce the cake all over with a metal skewer and loosen the cake from the sides of the tin.

Slowly pour half the syrup over the cake so that the syrup can gradually seep into the cake. Stand 10 minutes and repeat. Once cold, turn the savarin onto a cake plate to serve. Fill the centre with whipped sweetened cream and fresh berries.

syrup
Put the sugar, water and vanilla essence into a saucepan and stir over a low heat until the sugar has dissolved. Stir in Kirsch, liqueur or fruit juice. Allow to cool.

Twas the night before Christmas,
When all through the house,
Not a creature was stirring,
Not even a mouse.
The stockings were hung
By the chimney with care,
In the hopes that Saint Nicholas soon would be there:
The children have nestled
All snug in their beds,
While visions of sugar-plums
Dance in their heads…

– From *A Visit from Saint Nicholas* by Clement C. Moore

allyson's tip

↳ If left to go stale, this is wonderful toasted and buttered.

- 1 cup sultanas or currants, or a mix of both
- 2 tablespoons brandy
- 3 cups high grade flour
- 3 tablespoons caster sugar
- ¼ cup mixed peel
- ¼ cup sliced almonds

- ¼ cup finely chopped papaya or mixed peel
- 1 cup milk, warm
- 1 teaspoon caster sugar
- 2 teaspoons active dry yeast or 2 tablespoons Surebake yeast mix

- 1 egg
- 75 grams butter, melted
- 1 tablespoon butter, softened
- 200 grams marzipan
- rosewater to flavour

butter & sugar coating
- 50 grams butter, melted
- ½ cup icing sugar

christstollen

makes 1 large loaf, serves 10–12
preparation time 2¾ hours
cooking time 45–50 minutes

This German Christmas cake is traditionally eaten during Advent in Germany. The Christstollen has a marzipan heart that represents baby Jesus and the cake is the blanket in which he was wrapped.

Toss the sultanas or currants in the brandy and set aside for 1 hour.

Sift flour and a pinch of salt together. Take 1 cup of flour and set aside. To the remaining 2 cups of flour, add the 3 tablespoons caster sugar, mixed peel, almonds, papaya or mixed peel and sultanas or currants. Set aside.

Stir the warm milk, sugar and yeast together and set aside for 10 minutes, or until the mixture is frothy.

To the 1 cup of flour add the yeasty liquid, egg and melted butter and beat well to achieve a smooth batter. Cover with a clean tea towel or plastic wrap. Stand in a warm place for 40 minutes or until the batter has doubled in bulk and is bubbly.

Stir this mixture into the flour and fruit mixture and mix to a firm dough. Turn out onto a floured surface and knead for about 10 minutes until smooth.

Turn dough over in a well-greased bowl and spread the softened butter over the top of the dough. Cover with

plastic wrap and set aside in a warm place for one hour or until double in bulk.

Turn the dough out onto a floured surface and gently press the dough down to deflate. Roll the dough into a large oval, about 1½-cm thick.

Knead the marzipan with a little rosewater to flavour. Roll the marzipan out to form a thick sausage the length of the dough and place it right of centre. Brush the edge of the dough with milk. Fold the dough over the marzipan to make an oval semi-circle and press the edges together firmly.

Transfer to a greased baking tray. Cover with a clean lightweight tea towel and set aside in a warm place for about 40 minutes until the dough has doubled in bulk.

Preheat the oven to 200 °C. Bake in the preheated oven for 10 minutes, then lower the oven to 180 °C for a further 35–40 minutes until golden. The dough is cooked when it sounds hollow when tapped underneath. Transfer the Stollen onto a cake rack to cool.

For the butter and sugar coating brush the warm Stollen well with the butter and sift the icing sugar liberally on top. Serve cut in slices.

1¼ teaspoons active dry yeast
   or 4 teaspoons Surebake
   yeast mix
1¼ cups warm water
2 tablespoons virgin olive oil
3 cups high grade flour
1 teaspoon salt
1 tablespoon sugar

100 grams grapes, green or
   black
¾ cup walnuts, chopped
   roughly
4–6 sprigs fresh rosemary,
   chopped roughly
¼ cup virgin olive oil

focaccia

makes 2 loaves
preparation time **2 hours**
cooking time **20 minutes**

Sprinkle the yeast over the water and stir in the first measure of olive oil with a pinch of sugar. Leave in a warm place for 10 minutes or until the mixture is frothy.

Put the flour, salt and sugar into a food processor and pulse to sift.

Turn the food processor on. Pour the frothy yeast liquid slowly down the feed tube and process the soft dough for 1 minute. Add more liquid if necessary. The dough should run around the bowl in one ball and not stick to the sides of the bowl.

Bring the dough together on a floured surface. Place into a large greased bowl, turn over and cover with greased plastic wrap. Leave in a warm place for one hour or until double in bulk.

Turn the dough out onto a lightly floured surface. Divide in half and roll each half out to a 20–23-cm round or square and place on a greased baking tray or, if wished, into greased cake tins. Cover with a clean tea towel and set aside for 20 minutes.

Press the tips of your fingers into the dough to make the traditional focaccia dents. Press the grapes into these dents and scatter the walnuts, rosemary and the second measure of oil evenly over each focaccia. Rest a further 10 minutes.

Preheat the oven to 220 °C.

Bake for 20 minutes or until golden brown and crisp. Serve warm drizzled with extra olive oil and sprinkled with flaky salt and fresh rosemary.

to make by hand
Sponge the yeast as outlined in step 1. Sift the flour, salt and sugar into a large bowl and make a well in the centre. Gradually mix in the frothy yeast mixture and when all the flour is almost absorbed, turn the dough out onto a lightly floured surface and knead well for 10 minutes until the dough is smooth. Continue as above.

variation
❧ Use half wholemeal and half plain flour.

All sorrows are less with bread.
– Miguel de Cervantes, *Don Quixote*

2 teaspoons active dry yeast
   or 2 tablespoons Surebake
   yeast mix
1 teaspoon sugar
1¼ cups milk, warm
3½ cups high grade flour
½ cup caster sugar

75 grams butter, softened
½ teaspoon salt
2 eggs, separated
1 teaspoon vanilla essence
extra milk to glaze

nut & fruit filling
¾ cup ground almonds
½ cup sultanas
¼ cup finely chopped glacé
   cherries
¼ cup sugar

sweet easter bread

makes 1 large loaf
preparation time **3 hours**
cooking time **45 minutes**

Delicious made 5–6 days in advance of eating and served toasted for a special brunch.

Stir the yeast and the 1 teaspoon sugar into the milk and leave for 10–12 minutes or until slightly frothy. Beat in 1 cup of the flour and stand for a further 5 minutes in a warm place until the batter is frothy again.

In a food processor, put the remaining flour the ½ cup sugar, half the butter and the salt and process until the mixture resembles crumbs.

Add the egg yolks and vanilla essence to the frothy yeast mixture and with the motor running pour all the yeast mixture into the processor as fast as the flour can absorb it, adding more milk if necessary to make a soft dough. Process for 1 minute.

Transfer the dough to a greased bowl. Turn over and cover with plastic wrap. Put in a warm place for an hour or until double in bulk.

Whip the egg whites with a fork until broken down and lightly frothy. Stir in the filling ingredients.

Turn out the dough and gently push down to deflate. Roll out the dough to an oblong 1½-cm thick, about 40 cm x 30 cm in size.

Spread the remaining butter over the dough then carefully spread over the almond and cherry mix.

Roll up from the long side ensuring the join is on the bottom and the ends are well pinched together.

Place the loaf on a greased tray. Cover with a lightweight clean tea towel, and leave in a warm place for 45 minutes or until double in bulk.

Preheat the oven to 190 °C.

Once double in bulk, glaze with milk and bake in the preheated oven for 45 minutes, or until the loaf sounds hollow when tapped underneath.

Transfer to a cake rack to cool. Spread with a little butter and sift icing sugar over the loaf, if wished, before it cools completely. Slice thickly.

to make by hand

Sponge the yeast as outlined in step 1. Sift the remaining flour, sugar and salt into a large bowl and rub in half the butter. Make a well in the centre. Add the egg yolks to the frothy yeast mixture and begin to work into the flour. Once almost all the flour has been absorbed, turn the dough out onto a lightly floured surface and knead well for 10 minutes until the dough is smooth. Continue as above.

And the Qangle Wangle said
To himself on the crumpety tree
'Jam and Jelly and bread
Are the best of foods for me'.
– Edward Lear

2 teaspoons active dry yeast
  or 6 teaspoons Surebake
  yeast mix
¼ cup warm water
½ teaspoon sugar
4½ cups high grade flour
2 teaspoons salt
about 1¾ cups cold tap water

baker's white bread

makes 1 large loaf
preparation time **3 hours**
cooking time **35–40 minutes**

Most bread machines come with a standard bread recipe that can also be made by hand – here's my favourite recipe. It takes a little longer to make, with extra resting times, but the end product is sensational. It makes a wonderful large loaf that is delicious fresh or toasted a few days later.

Mix the yeast, water and sugar together and set aside for about 3 minutes until the yeast dissolves and becomes slightly frothy. (If you are using Surebake yeast, the mixture will become porridge-like.)

Sift the flour and salt into a large bowl and make a well in the centre.

Pour in the yeasty liquid and half of the second measure of water. Mix with one hand, adding more water as needed to form a sticky mass.

Turn out onto a lightly floured surface and just bring together. It will look untidy. Cover with a clean, slightly dampened tea towel and leave for 10–15 minutes.

Knead for about 7–10 minutes until the dough is supple, using very little flour to dust the bench.

Transfer to a greased bowl and brush the top of the dough with oil. Cover with plastic wrap and then a warm towel and stand aside until it has doubled in bulk. In summer this may take 1½ hours and in winter up to 2½ hours.

Turn the dough out and knead gently to deflate. Bring all the outside edges into the centre and then turn the dough over so that the top is smooth side up. Work the dough in a circular motion, moulding it into a large ball.

Place the ball smooth side uppermost into a calico-lined basket or greased and well-floured bowl. Dust the top with flour. Cover with plastic wrap and set aside for about 45–60 minutes until the dough has doubled in size.

Set the oven rack to the middle or just below the middle of the oven. Preheat the oven to 200 °C.

Once doubled you will need to work quickly. Turn the dough upside down onto a well-floured baking tray. Sift a liberal layer of flour over the top to make a good covering. Do not be alarmed if the dough begins to open as the smooth side is tray side down. This will give you a fabulous uneven patterned top.

Bake in the preheated oven for 35–40 minutes until the loaf is well risen, brown and sounds hollow when tapped from underneath. Transfer to a cake rack to cool.

allyson's tip

❧ You can prepare the dough in the bread machine and then shape into buns or shape into the loaves, leave to rest until doubled in size and bake in the oven.

- ¾ cup raisins or dried cherries
- 2 tablespoons dark rum
- 1½ teaspoons active dry yeast or 5 teaspoons Surebake yeast mix
- ¼ cup warm water
- 2 tablespoons honey
- 3½ cups high grade flour
- ½ cup cocoa
- 2 teaspoons salt
- ¼ cup caster sugar
- 1¼ cups cold water
- 75 grams butter, softened
- ½ cup chocolate chips

chocolate raisin bread

makes 12 buns or 2 loaves
preparation time 2½ hours
cooking time 25 minutes for buns or 40 minutes for a loaf

Delicious served toasted and spread with cream cheese and cherry jam.

Mix the raisins or dried cherries and rum together and set aside.

Stir the yeast into the water with the honey and set aside for about 3 minutes until the yeast dissolves and becomes slightly frothy. (If you are using Surebake this will become porridge-like.)

Sift the flour, cocoa, salt and sugar into a large bowl and make a well in the centre.

Pour the yeasty liquid into the well and almost all the second measure of water. Mix with one hand adding more water if needed to form a sticky mass.

Turn out onto a lightly floured surface and just bring together. It will look untidy. Cover with a clean tea towel and leave for 10–15 minutes.

Push the dough out a little and spread the butter, chocolate chips and raisins and rum on top. Fold the dough up like a three-folded business letter and begin to knead. It will look incredibly untidy and seem to almost separate into sections. Just keep kneading until you have a smooth supple dough. Dust the bench with flour only when needed.

Transfer to a greased bowl, cover with greased plastic wrap and a towel and stand aside in a warm place until double in bulk.

Turn the dough out and deflate gently.

For buns, divide the mixture into 12 even-sized portions and knead each into a smooth ball. Place the buns on a greased tray about 1 cm apart, smooth side up. Cover with greased plastic wrap and set aside for 40 minutes until double in bulk.

For loaves, divide the dough in half and mould into two loaves. Place into two well-greased medium-sized (22-cm x 9-cm) loaf tins. Cover with greased plastic wrap and set aside for 45–50 minutes until double in bulk.

Place the oven rack in the middle of the oven. Preheat the oven to 200 °C.

Once the dough has doubled, bake in the preheated oven for 20–25 minutes for buns and about 40 minutes for the loaves. The bread should sound hollow when tapped from underneath. Transfer to a cake rack to cool. Decorate the top with sifted icing sugar, if wished.

1¼ teaspoons active dry yeast
   or 4 teaspoons Surebake
   yeast mix
1 cup warm water or milk
1 teaspoon sugar
1½ cup high grade flour
1 cup wholemeal flour

1 teaspoon salt
50 grams butter, softened
2 tablespoons treacle or golden
   syrup
¼–½ cup linseeds

topping ideas
¼ cup linseeds, oat flakes,
   oat bran, pumpkin seeds
   or sunflower seeds or a
   mixture of these

one-rise linseed bread

makes 1 loaf
preparation time **1½ hours**
cooking time **30–35 minutes**

This is a favourite one-rise recipe in my home. Rising bread twice will ensure a finer texture, but often we want a quick-to-make loaf. Try this one packed with linseeds and sweetened with treacle.

Grease and flour a medium-sized (22-cm x 9-cm) loaf tin.

Stir the yeast into the warm water and sugar and set aside for 10–12 minutes until frothy.

Put the flour, wholemeal flour and salt into a food processor and pulse to sift. Add the butter and process until rubbed in.

Add the treacle or golden syrup to the frothy yeast mixture.

Turn on the food processor. Pour the liquid slowly down the feed tube to form a soft dough. Add any extra water if required. The mixture should be moist.

Quickly pulse in the linseeds.

Transfer the dough into the prepared loaf tin. Sprinkle over one of the suggested topping ingredients.

Cover loosely with greased plastic wrap and wrap in a towel. Leave in a warm place for 1 hour or until the loaf is double in bulk.

While rising preheat the oven to 200 °C.

Bake in the preheated oven for 30–35 minutes or until the loaf sounds hollow when tapped underneath. Remove from the oven and transfer quickly to a cake rack to cool.

to make by hand
Sponge the yeast as described in step 2. Add the treacle or golden syrup. Sift the flours and salt into a bowl. Rub in the butter and stir through the linseeds. Make a well in the centre and gradually pour in the frothy yeast mixture. Once most of the flour has been absorbed, turn the dough out onto a lightly floured bench and knead well for 10 minutes until the dough is smooth. Place into the prepared tin and continue as above.

variation
- In place of linseeds use pumpkin seeds, sunflower seeds or a combination of them.

¾ cup warm water
2 tablespoons sugar
1½ teaspoons active dry yeast
3¾ cups high grade flour
2 teaspoons salt
2 eggs
125 grams butter, softened

almond topping
100 grams butter
¼ cup honey
¼ cup sugar
2 tablespoons glucose or corn syrup
grated rind of 1 lemon,
grated rind of 1 small orange
1–1½ cups sliced almonds

custard cream
3 egg yolks
¼ cup caster sugar
3 tablespoons flour
1 cup whole milk or cream
1 teaspoon vanilla or lemon essence

gateau bernard

serves **12**
preparation time **3½ hours**
cooking time **30–35 minutes**

Stir the warm water and 1 tablespoon of the sugar together until the sugar dissolves. Stir in the yeast and leave for 10 minutes until the mixture becomes quite frothy.

Sift the flour, salt and remaining sugar into a mix master fitted with the K beater and make a well in the centre. Add the frothy mixture, eggs and butter and beat on a medium speed for 6 minutes. The dough will come together to form a soft pliable mass.

Turn out, and place into a well-greased bowl and cover with plastic wrap. Stand in a warm place for about 1½–2 hours or until the dough has doubled in bulk. Do not hurry the rising as the slower the rise, the better the flavour and texture of the finished product.

Turn the dough out onto a lightly floured surface and knead lightly. Press into a well-greased and lined 30-cm round cake tin.

Spread the slightly warm topping gently over the top of the dough. Cover the cake or cake tin loosely with plastic wrap and leave in a warm place until the dough doubles in size again. This second rise will take about 1 hour.

Place the oven rack in the middle of the oven. Preheat the oven to 180 °C.

Once the dough has risen, bake in the preheated oven for 30–35 minutes or until the dough is well risen and firm to the touch in the centre.

Remove from the oven and leave to cool for 10 minutes before turning out and transferring to a cake rack. Be careful as the topping is scalding hot.

When cool, split in half horizontally and fill with the custard cream. Serve in wedges.

almond topping
In a saucepan, stir the butter, honey, sugar, syrup and citrus rinds over a gentle heat until the sugar has dissolved. Bring to the boil, remove from the heat and stir in the almonds. Cool. Keep in a lidded container in a cool part of the kitchen if making in advance.

custard cream
Combine the egg yolks, sugar, flour, milk or cream and essence together in a saucepan and stir over a moderate heat until the custard mixture becomes very thick. Butter a piece of baking paper and place it buttered-side-down on top of the custard and set it to cool. Keep refrigerated in an airtight container if making in advance.

glossary

bain marie/water bath
To create a water bath you need a large pan of hot water into which you place a smaller dish to heat or cook its contents. I use a roasting dish to act as a water bath. It is a slow gentle way of cooking foods, such as baked custards.

Fill the water bath up with water once you have both dishes in the oven. Do not try to carry a large open dish of water to the oven as it has a tendency to gather momentum and the water spills out.

Likewise when removing the dish, remove the dessert and allow the water bath to cool first if you can before taking it from the oven. And be careful!

baking blind
Is where the pastry for a tart or flan is cooked prior to the filling be added. This allows the pastry to cook and not become soggy. Line the tin with pastry and prick the base with the tines of a fork. Line with baking paper and fill with baking blind beans to weigh down the pastry when cooking.

baking blind beans
Are lightweight aluminium beans, rice or dried beans, which are used to weigh down pastry when baking blind. The beans can be used repeatedly.

beating
Mixing vigorously to blend ingredients together or to create lightness through aerating a mixture.

biscuit forcer
A small cylinder into which raw biscuit mixture can be placed and pushed down with a plunger or lever through patterned discs at the base to create intricate patterned biscuits.

cake rack
An open-grid, metal stand for cooling baking on. Those with higher legs allow for a more even air flow.

cream (to)
To beat or work butter and sugar together until it is light in colour and texture.

Correctly creamed, the mixture should be almost twice its original volume.

egg wash/egg glaze
A glaze made from one egg yolk and 2 tablespoons water. Used to brush on goods before baking (where indicated) to achieve a golden colour to the finished goods.

fold (to)
To very lightly incorporate two or three mixtures together without losing any air that has been incorporated in the beating process. Folding with your hand or a slotted spoon is best.

knead (to)
To work a dough or pastry to ensure an even-textured mass. To achieve this press the dough or pastry down with the heel of your hand. Lift up about $1/3$ of the dough farthest away from you and fold over in the centre of the mass and then push down with the heel of your hand. Give the dough or pastry a quarter turn and repeat. Do not turn the dough over and always knead into the middle on the same side.

loose-bottom cake tin
Literally, a cake tin where the base is loose, as opposed to a spring-form cake tin.

make a well
To push the flour or other dry ingredients to the edge of the bowl and make a deep well in the centre into which wet ingredients are added and gradually incorporated. Done slowly, as when making pancakes, the end batter should have no flour lumps.

preheated
To heat the oven well in advance of placing the goods in to be baked. Baking should never be placed into a cold oven, unless otherwise stated, as the end result will be disappointing.

proving
This is the first resting given to yeast-baked dough after kneading. It allows the dough to relax and the yeast to begin its work. A dough is proven sufficiently when you press you finger gently into the centre and the indent remains.

pulse (food processor)
To mix by turning the food processor on and off. This ensures even chopping of dry goods such as nuts and avoids over-mixing items such as pastry.

sift
To put dry foods into a fine-meshed sieve or flour sifter and shake through to ensure even mixing of dry ingredients and to remove any other unwanted matter.

skewer
A thin metal stick or bamboo stick used to insert into baked goods to test for doneness. Pierce into the centre of the cake and if any raw, uncooked mixture remains clinging to the skewer the cake requires further baking time.

soft thick peaks (egg whites)
Is when you lift the beaters from a mixture of beaten egg whites, or egg whites and sugar, and the peak of the mixture falls over.

spring-form cake tin
A cake tin where the sides extend to allow the base to drop out.

tines
The prongs on the end of a fork.

your notes

....
....
....
....
....
....
....
....
....
....
....
....
....
....

WEDNESDAY

your notes

....
....
....
....
....
....
....
....
....
....
....
....
....
....

SATURDAY

your notes

....
....
....
....
....
....
....
....
....
....
....
....
....
....
....
....

SUNDAY

index